Advance Praise for

THE TRADE GAP

If you've gotten too comfortable behind a screen, The Trade Gap is your gritty, practical guide to reclaiming purpose through real, hands-on skills.

—**MICHAEL EASTER**, New York Times Bestselling Author of The Comfort Crisis

The Trade Gap is a compelling call to arms, urging Americans to rediscover the value of skilled trades in an age that's forgotten the power of practical know-how. Well worth the read!

—**NELSON DELLIS**, 6x USA Memory Champion and Multiple Best-Selling Author

It isn't easy walking away from comfort but Zach Hanson explains the expectations and ultimate rewards from following your heart's passions. This book is a must-read for those ready to make a leap of faith toward their dreams.

—**KEVIN ESTELA**, Owner and Chief Survival Instructor at Kevin Estela, LLC

A much-needed wake-up call! Hanson dives into how America's focus on knowledge work has left us unprepared for the basics—building, fixing, and keeping things running. Through personal stories and history, he makes a strong case for bringing back hands-on skills and trades education. A must-read for those who value the trades or want to rediscover the power of working with their hands.

—**BRIANA HUHN**, Founder of
Huhny Bee Tools & Trades

The Trade Gap is a sobering picture of where the United States and most of the modern world have slipped into a dependent lifestyle with a limited number of trade workers that bear the weight of the nation on their shoulders.

—**HUGH RAE**, Journeyman Lineman and
Owner of Blunt Force Karma LLC

There is literally no downside to being self-reliant. This book should be required reading for all 16-year-olds in the country. More so, it should be required reading for their parents. The impact of devaluing vocational trades and basic maintenance knowledge in America is evident today with fewer young men and women having the skills to perform minimal tasks at home, let alone as a career. This book conveys to the reader just how tenuous that circumstance can make our society.

—**PHILLIP REPEPPI**, CEO, LOSO Backpack Company & Wanayi Camouflage Company

From job security to national security to insecurity, Zach shows how we all benefit from being more capable and self-reliant as individuals and as a whole.

—**MICAH HAZEN**, Journeyman Electrician and Owner of Eagle Electric & Lighting

In *The Trade Gap*, Zach Hanson provides a fantastic introduction into the skilled trade challenges in our society today. Would recommend for anyone passionate about empowering the nation's workforce and building a happier, wealthier America.

—**RUCHIR SHAH**, CEO of SkillCat

The Trade Gap is about more than fixing a broken system—it's about fixing ourselves. Zach's story hits home for anyone who's looked around at their comfortable life and realized their so-called "skills" don't produce anything real. That comfort? It's propped up by a shrinking group of people living a very different kind of life. This book is a reminder that real confidence comes from competence—and that starts with learning to work with your hands. There's no workaround.

—**CLIFF GRAY**, Hunting Guide &
Host of Pursuit with Cliff

THE
TRADE
GAP

**BREAK THE RULES. LEARN A SKILL.
OWN YOUR FUTURE.**

ZACHARY CRAIG HANSON

WREN HOUSE
press

THE TRADE GAP
Break the Rules. Learn a Skill. Own Your Future.
First Edition

ISBN   978-1-967115-11-2   *Hardcover*
           978-1-967115-09-9   *Paperback*
           978-1-967115-10-5   *Ebook*

LCCN 2025912255

For my grandparents, who have always supported me, my writing, and my growing family. My grandfather—still welding at eighty-eight—proves that real skill and dedication have no expiration date. This book is a testament to bridging the trade gap and carrying forward our legacy of discipline, craftsmanship, and hard work for generations to come.

"[A]nd to make it your ambition to lead a quiet life: You should mind your own business and work with your hands, just as we told you, so that your daily life may win the respect of outsiders and so that you will not be dependent on anybody."

—1 Thessalonians 4:11–12 (NIV)

CONTENTS

FOREWORD

by NICK UHAS

As a millennial, I often felt a sense of skepticism whenever I heard the words "trade" or "trade school." Where I came from in the Midwest, these words were commonly synonymous with "underachievement"— an idea that pursuing a trade was somehow a lesser path than going to college. But my own journey has shown me just how wrong that view is. In fact, without the practical skills I gained in the trades, I wouldn't be where I am today.

Whether it's hanging drywall, painting a wall, fixing a leaky toilet, or climbing up on a roof to patch a hole, these basic yet invaluable skills have been essential to my personal and professional growth. To many people, these skills seem outdated, like some kind of vestigial organ we no longer need. But in *The Trade Gap*, Zach Hanson powerfully argues why the trades are far from obsolete. With clarity and precision, he outlines the importance of these skills and how they serve as the foundational knowledge we all need to build upon.

Through Zach's life experience, we begin to see the trades in a new light. For those of us who grew up with the conventional wisdom of "go to college, then get a good job," Zach's perspective is a refreshing and much-needed challenge to that outdated narrative. I believe what Zach has captured in these pages reflects questions many of us have asked ourselves: *Why is it that someone with a two-year degree in the trades can often outearn someone with a master's degree or even a PhD? Isn't there a better way to approach work and life?*

Even more importantly, he presents a better, more logical path forward—a path that not only benefits the individual but also holds the potential to reshape the future of American society.

I'm confident that, after reading this book, you'll walk away with a renewed sense of purpose and the desire to pick up the tools that have been missing from your own life. *The Trade Gap* will inspire you to rethink what's truly valuable—and to see why the skills described in these pages are not just useful but actually the key to unlocking a future filled with opportunity, self-sufficiency, and success.

—Nick Uhas
Media Entrepreneur

INTRODUCTION

There's something deeply unsettling about realizing that everything you depend on—your comfort, your security, your success—is built on things you cannot fix. Your fancy car? Useless if it breaks down. The security cameras in your high-tech home? Another piece of junk if your internet provider goes down. It's easy to live in this bubble until, one day, it bursts—and you're left standing in a kitchen that's just lost power, staring at the reality that you have no idea how to even begin solving the problem.

This was me. I was living the American dream—or so I thought. I'd worked hard, I'd earned degrees, and with a lot of grit, I had landed a well-paying job in the knowledge economy. On paper, everything was perfect. But under the surface, I was trapped. The truth hit me one morning as I stared at the useless gadgets and appliances around me: If anything went seriously wrong, I wouldn't know how to fix it. Worse yet, I wouldn't be able to provide for my family in any meaningful way if the grid went down, the economy tanked, or we faced a real national crisis. I was a prisoner of my own ignorance.

My first real step toward change came when I found myself sitting in a welding booth at a local community college in my mid-thirties. Surrounded by people half my age or twice as old, I was well educated and utterly clueless. I clicked my pen nervously, just as I had done in graduate school, but this time the stakes felt different. I wasn't there to memorize theories or write papers; I was there to learn something real. To build. To create. To fix.

When my instructor, Marty, shoved a welding electrode into my hand and said, "Let's start a weld... tack those pieces together," it was like stepping into a different world. The crackle of electricity, the bright flash of molten metal fusing together—it was a kind of magic I had never experienced in my years as a white-collar worker. After laying my first few terrible welds, something inside me shifted. I wasn't just a guy who sat in digital meetings and pecked out emails. I was a guy who could take two pieces of metal and make them one.

The experience of learning to weld wasn't just about metalwork. It was also about rebuilding myself. I realized what I'd been taught—that success was measured by degrees and office titles—was only part of the equation. The other part was far more primal: the ability to create, repair, and survive with my own hands.

This book is about why that journey isn't just necessary for me—it's necessary for every American. We've built a society where fewer and fewer people know how to create, maintain, or repair the very things that sustain our everyday lives. And it's a crisis in the making.

In a world where artificial intelligence is replacing jobs we thought were safe and skilled trades are becoming increasingly rare and valuable, the divide between those who know how to work with their hands and those who don't is growing. The future belongs to people who can adapt, who can pivot when the world shifts beneath their feet. And to do that, you need skills that go beyond what they teach in classrooms.

1
ORIGINS OF PRACTICAL INVENTION

I N WHAT IS NOW IRAQ, THE PEOPLE OF MES-opotamia invented the wheel around the fourth millennium BC. Initially created for pottery spinning, artisans played around with inserting solid axles into wooden discs to speed up the rate at which they could mold clay into items for everyday use and survival. It would take roughly another thousand years before someone thought to flip one of those discs on its side and roll it around on the ground. I like to imagine a clumsy Mesopotamian bumping into one of their pottery wheels and knocking it on its side. As it hits the ground and rolls around its axle, it slowly comes to a halt against the wall. Looking down, the Mesopotamian has an "aha" moment, realizing they could potentially use the wheel as a means to roll their goods to market with more ease. This kicks off a chain reaction of experimentation that leads to a basic cart, which in turn changes the landscape of war, transportation, and agriculture forever.

Did the discovery of the wheel really happen in this way? Probably not—at least not in the exact comedic scenario I laid out, but the underlying concept of discovery holds. For most of human history, major discoveries and inventions have come about through practical, hands-on experience and experimentation, usually tied to a core need for survival. Most humans did not sit around theorizing or go through focused scholarly training before trying and discovering something new.

The Mesopotamian artisans who invented the wheel likely didn't sit for hours on end thinking of the best way to capture the power of centrifugal force to ease the burden of their clay-making task. Nor did they draft blueprints of their design over and over again until they got it perfect before hammering out a crude wheel.

The reality is that for most of known history, humans have learned by trial and error—we were not the thinking man; we were the doing man. Yes, the invention of the wheel emerged the same way cavemen discovered fire: through keen observation and a desire to capture the energy of something unknown. That desire to tame elements of the natural world, enhance them, and leverage them to make daily life easier is the tale of human evolution.

From the cavemen to Thomas Edison, inventors rarely had a full picture of the theory underlying their pursuit. They were all working from a limited or even false knowledge base that forced them to experiment with what worked—and more importantly, what didn't work.

This is how the Egyptians discovered glass. They observed melting sand that cooled into a transparent rock and realized they could leverage it for myriad purposes. It's how Chinese alchemists accidentally discovered gunpowder while searching for an elixir to help them live longer. By combining charcoal, saltpeter, and sulfur, they somehow found that this new mix was extremely combustible and could be better used for ending life instead of extending it.

When Thomas Edison played with different filaments for his light bulb, he had no ChatGPT to consult when questions arose. Instead, he experimented until he found something that worked. When Elihu Thomson struck the first electric arc to be used for welding, he surely didn't understand every gas and electron movement happening within the flash that sparked before him. No, for every historic invention, practical interaction and hands-on play was the driving force. Deep theoretical understanding of the invention came later.

This age-old process has led to a more unsettling trend that has repeated itself throughout human history as well. As societies and cultures have risen around inventions, there always seems to be an over indexing on the theoretical study of the things, at the expense of continued practical experience.

In ancient Rome, toward the end of the empire, the main value marker for success among nobility and the elites was to be classically educated with a focus on oratory and philosophical discourse. The rates of broad education in military training, craftsmanship, and engineering took a nosedive, which ultimately led to porous borders, failing infrastructure, the outsourcing of trade work to foreigners, and the reliance on foreign military for protection. The push for intellectual study failed to equip the last generation of Romans with the skills needed to deal with daily practical challenges, which was a key contributing factor to Rome's ultimate demise.

Confucian China, the Byzantine Empire, Renaissance Italy, and even the ancient Islamic world met a similar demise—all empires that at some point tipped the educational scales in favor of less practical and more theoretical study. These empires opened themselves up to economic, political, and military vulnerabilities that prodded them in the direction of self-destruction.

Today, the American experiment is at clear risk of repeating the same mistakes as these great empires of the past. Like them, we have placed a societal value on the pursuit of specialized knowledge work, not in conjunction with practical, hands-on education

but seemingly in opposition to it. We have success-
fully redirected American students toward allegedly
more valuable intellectual industries, at the expense
of building a base of students who have a keen interest in keeping our country running. For the last four
decades, there has been a war on tradespeople and
skilled workers. The cultural message has been that
learning to be a lineman, an electrician, a butcher, a
construction worker, a sanitation worker, or a spe-
cialist in any skill that does not require a four-year
university degree is an admission of failure.

As we move into the next phase of technological advancements and the winnowing of digital jobs
increases, there is a collective "uh-oh" rising among
the elites in our country. That's because—not unlike
Rome, the Byzantine Empire, or dynasties throughout
Confucian China—we are now a country full of over-
educated individuals who have nearly zero practical
skills. Like those failed empires, we must outsource
much of what we need done to continue supporting
our country. We are seeing our military dominance
decline and our state and local infrastructure fail. And
as technology and AI replace the jobs of knowledge

workers, we are left with a mass of people lacking in valuable skills, people who can no longer contribute to society in a meaningful way.

The decades-long educational push against the trades has eroded our country's founding principle of rugged individualism. For over a century, our public institutions taught the most basic skills of survival and self-reliance, but that's no longer the case. We have shunned the true knowledge of trade and craftsmanship, while coaching generations to rely on others for their basic needs. That works great—until it doesn't.

The buffer zone of comfort we've built for most citizens has disconnected them from the realities of providing warmth, creating shelter, and procuring food. Our society has created complex distribution systems on the heels of hard-nosed experimentation, and now people expect that these systems will always be around. However, without training new generations to maintain these systems, they *will* erode and go away just like the aqueducts and infrastructure of Rome.*

---

* Bryan Ward-Perkins, *The Fall of Rome: And the End of Civilization* (Oxford, England: Oxford University Press, 2005), 107.

How many young students today are apprenticing to become butchers who can provide sanitary protein options to the masses? How many teenagers know how to pour asphalt and concrete to repair our roads? What about students learning the ways of the roustabouts who know how to extract oil? How many adults even know how to change the oil in their own vehicles?

The answer to all of these questions is *very few*. If we know history repeats itself and our country was built by practical, blue-collar work, not theory alone, how did we end up in this predicament? To start teasing out an answer, we need to jump to more modern history.

2

THE DECLINE OF VOCATIONAL EDUCATION
HOW WE LOST OUR WAY

F YOU WERE BORN IN THE LATE '80S OR EARLY '90s, you were like me: lucky. That range of birth dates plops you into a generation now known as millennials—a generation that grew up in a relatively stable time in American economic history. Just take a look at the graph below from the Federal Reserve Economic Data (FRED),* depicting the total national public debt

---

* US Office of Management and Budget and Federal Reserve Bank of St. Louis, "Federal Debt: Total Public Debt as Percent...

as a percentage of our country's gross domestic product over a range of decades and generations.

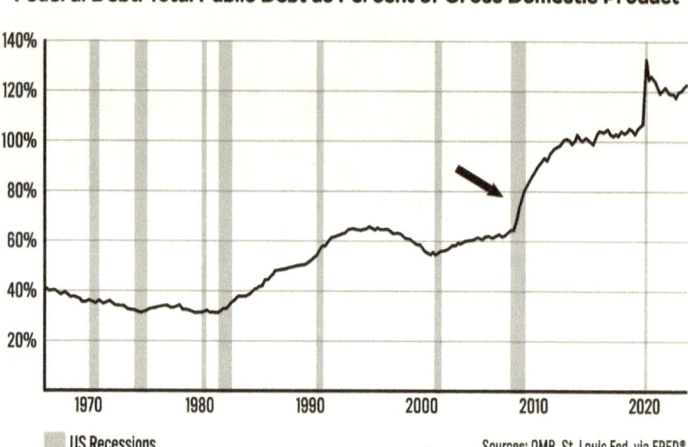

Federal Debt: Total Public Debt as Percent of Gross Domestic Product

US Recessions

Sources: OMB, St. Louis Fed, via FRED®

You can see that during the 1990s and early 2000s, as millennials were coming of age, the country was economically steady. Growth appeared unending, and the rise of the internet during our teen years stoked an already burning fire of seemingly unlimited potential.

...of Gross Domestic Product (GFDEGDQ188S)," FRED, https://fred.stlouisfed.org/series/GFDEGDQ188S.

For suburban families, it felt like everything our parents and grandparents had fought for was paying off, and it was truly an awesome time to grow up in the greatest nation in the world. The sustained economic stability leading into the new century gave us a sense that things would *always* be great. With that assurance came an idea that had started in the late '70s and early '80s: The path to success, the new American dream, ran through higher education and specialized knowledge careers.

The focus on university degrees during this period was palpable. As a kid, I remember middle school educators telling me that as long as I went to college and graduated, I would have a well-paying job—and I believed them.

I believe the advice was well intentioned, but understanding why it was *wrong* requires us to travel back in time—to the early twentieth century.

FEDERAL AID

In 1917, in the midst of World War I, two senators from the state of Georgia introduced the Smith–Hughes

National Vocational Education Act. The act was meant to address the economic depression in their home state due to record-high unemployment. They believed that investing in more training on modern agricultural practices and budding industrial technologies could help lift their fellow man out of the pit of destitution enveloping their state.

The Smith–Hughes Act became the first piece of federal legislation to promote trade and vocational education reform nationwide. Under the act, states had to match the available federal funding in order to receive it, which initially led to slow adoption. However, by 1920, every state had received and set up the appropriate vocational training centers, laying the groundwork for positioning America as the preeminent capitalist society with a nation of educated laborers. The act was augmented over the years by the George–Deen Act of 1936 and the George–Barden Act of 1946, to add support for new trades and vocations that cropped up during the Great Depression and after World War II, but the core of the Smith–Hughes Act remained largely untouched until the 1960s.

As times change, so do the needs of the country and the students it supports. The provisions required to accept funding from the Smith–Hughes Act were stringent and largely separated academic training from vocational training. Educators and legislators saw the changing world tide and believed students needed a well-rounded education in academic subjects, vocational skills, and budding industries such as technology, which is what the Vocational Education Act of 1963 aimed to do. It built on the foundation of the Smith–Hughes Act but gave states more flexibility in how they spent the funds and allowed them to tailor vocational education to local industries. It also pushed states to build out programs that combined vocational training with more stringent academic requirements, with the altruistic goal of graduating well-rounded students who possessed both practical skills and academic knowledge.

This was the education system that the baby boomer generation grew up in. My father remembers his shop classes, both wood and metal, that ultimately triggered him to pursue an engineering degree. He credits the practical training he received in shop class during middle school and high school as a key factor in helping him understand the more theoretical elements of engineering that he pursued at the university level. Plus, shop class had given him a set of skills that he could apply on the side to help fund his way through college.

In the 1960s and 1970s, America churned out students who could discuss the finer points of Kant and also fix a toilet—students who were well positioned to provide for their families after graduation from high school, whether or not they went on to pursue a university degree. It seemed the educational investment of the early twentieth century had come close to achieving its desired goals. That premise of producing well-rounded students seemed to hold true right up until the 1980s, when other countries began to catch up to our standard of education.

NATIONAL COMMISSION ON EXCELLENCE IN EDUCATION

In 1983, the National Commission on Excellence in Education released a scathing review of the American public education system titled *A Nation at Risk: The Imperative for Educational Reform.* The report exposed growing gaps in necessary education for the future workforce. Namely, it argued that technology was beginning to outpace the need for vocational training and that we should focus on educating "knowledge workers" who intended to enroll in four-year universities if we wanted to stay competitive on the world stage. The report galvanized legislators and led to the first real change in federal educational funding in close to eighty years.

The outcome was the slow withdrawal of funding from vocational training, redirecting the funds to more academic programming in order to raise standardized test scores and prepare students for university studies. This shift marked a concurrent change in attitudes; vocational training became a "less than desirable" economic path in our society. Throughout the late 1980s and into the 1990s, shop classes all but disappeared from most middle schools and high schools, with funds instead used to build computer labs to help shape the coming generation of millennial knowledge workers. Then in 2001, the No Child Left Behind Act was introduced. This act aimed to further shrink perceived disparities in education across the nation and raise national competitiveness by holding schools accountable for student performance. Unfortunately, the main focus remained college readiness, further cementing the cultural shift away from balanced vocational training.

By the time my generation entered the public education system, there were no metal- or woodworking shops to be found in most urban schools. From an early age, the emphasis was on basic computer literacy and performing well on standardized academic tests. Outside of the minimal vocational training I received from my dad and grandfather—like threading and sweating pipes, soldering, and performing basic home maintenance—I learned zero practical skills during my pre-university public education.

For my generation, it was all about the humanities and social and hard sciences—English, history, basic math, biology, and chemistry. Not a single class taught me basic life skills like how to balance a checkbook or how to do my taxes, and there was definitely no discussion of how to turn a wrench or change the oil in my car. The only thing my educators focused on was prep work for the college admission standardized tests.

In fact, as "motivation" to take college admissions seriously, one teacher in my high school civics class printed out a fake college application and placed it next to a hard hat on her desk. In front of her little "modern art" piece was a paper printout with the words "You Decide" in big, bold letters. In her mind, there was a right answer and a wrong answer. It was blatant.

Even though I grew up in a blue-collar town in the South, our public schools pushed the idea that going into trade work of any kind was a decision to be "less than." As a young and ambitious student, I took this message to heart. Over time, I began to push back against the physical labor my dad wanted me to do outside of school, replacing it with activities that I believed would get me into a decent four-year degree program.

I participated in mock trials, debate, theoretical pursuits like philosophy, and athletics. In fact, the only positive depiction of the trades in my sphere of influence came from a few television shows I enjoyed watching as a teenager. Mike Rowe's wildly successful show *Dirty Jobs* and a few car-related makeover shows like *Pimp My Ride* showcased a whole world of makers who represented the last bastion of skilled labor in the United States. The producers made this world seem accessible, exciting—and, dare I say, desirable. Yet none of the glitz and glamour of these tradespeople could counteract the gravitational pull of our education system's insistence on becoming a *knowledge worker*, and I never gave any real thought to pursuing a hands-on skill as a career.

In just one century, the US had completely transformed. We went from prioritizing trades in the early 1900s, to finding a strong balance between vocational and knowledge work throughout the '60s and '70s, to ultimately demonizing all trade work in the '90s and early 2000s.

When it came time for me to don the cap and gown and graduate from the American public high school education system, I felt ready—ready to transition into the next phase of the new American dream, which I was told required attending an expensive university.

3

NUMBERS BEHIND THE CRISIS

THE DECLINE OF SKILLED TRADES

OR MY GENERATION, IT WAS COLLEGE OR bust. Yet one thing the public education system did not prepare any of us for was the competition involved in getting admitted to a decent university. The countrywide system produced so many college-bound students that the odds of receiving an acceptance letter from a great school were extremely low. Of the college-bound students I graduated with in 2007, only about 4 percent were headed for top-tier Ivy League schools.

So where did everyone else go? Like myself, 67 percent wound up at one of the many different state and local colleges. This isn't a bad thing in and of itself, but considering the average price of in-state tuition was $6,200 per year and out-of-state tuition fees averaged $16,600 per year for midrange public colleges, we had unknowingly entered the era of pay-to-play education.

On the flip side, just 5 to 7 percent of all high schoolers nationwide who graduated the year I did, in 2007, bucked the system and pursued vocational and trade education. This means that out of 3.3 million students, around 2.3 million were directly fed into a system where they took on massive debt for career education that did not teach hands-on skills, while approximately 200,000 pursued less expensive and more in-demand trade work.*

---

* Institute of Education Sciences, "Estimated Rate of 2007–08 High School Graduates Attending Degree-Granting Institutions, by State: 2008," Digest of Education Statistics, accessed Nov. 19, 2024, https://nces.ed.gov/programs/digest/d11/tables/dt11_212.asp.

Think about that for a moment. In just one graduating year, only 200,000 students *nationwide* pursued the trades that keep this country running, learning to fill roles including truck drivers, welders, plumbers, electricians, butchers, mechanics, fabricators, and other makers. It's not hard to see that with this yearly ratio of college-bound students to tradespeople, we were on a collision course with chaos. Yet except for a few prominent voices like Mike Rowe acting as modern-day Paul Reveres, the warnings largely fell on deaf ears.

CHINA

In 1983, the same year America released *A Nation at Risk*, China was emerging from its Cultural Revolution. In similar fashion to the United States, educational reform was top of mind, and the Chinese were set on building a plan that would make them a global powerhouse of industry.

A key part of that plan centered around reforming primary education. With the vast majority of the country being rural, China's main goals were to ensure that every person had the chance to receive an education and to raise the general literacy rate. Leader Deng Xiaoping wanted China to become proficient across agriculture, industry, defense, science, and technology.

To ensure a balance among these arenas, the educational system emphasized having exposure to and build base skills in each one, no matter a student's chosen specialty. Like the US, China realized early that prioritizing STEM-related workers was key to long-term success, but the Chinese government also recognized that investing in technology could not come at the expense of producing workers in the trades. Furthermore, it understood that technology would outpace and eventually become a part of trade education. Early on, the Chinese government set multiyear checkpoints for vocational schools to ensure that students also received training on the most modern technology that applied to their trade.

Now, this is by no means an endorsement of China's Democratic Socialist Party, but it is a nod to the broader educational philosophy. If I were to put it in terms many Americans would understand, it's akin to the modus operandi of the US Marines. Their mantra is "Every Marine a rifleman," meaning that every member of the Corps must possess a certain baseline of skill, no matter their specialized job function. We as Americans have gotten away from that kind of well-rounded education. We've put all our eggs into the basket of knowledge-work specialization, without considering the consequences.

THE INVISIBLE HAND

To steer away from socialism and back toward my support of laissez-faire economics and free-market capitalism, I think it's important to understand the larger impacts of our recent educational decision-making as a country. In a 1958 essay titled "I, Pencil," Leonard Read explains why the most basic commodity of his time, the number 2 pencil, was actually way more complex than most people realized. Made up of four basic components—cedar, graphite, rubber, and metal—a pencil seemed easy to construct and offer at a controlled price.

Yet as Read digs deeper, he details the vast "family tree" related to each of the pencil's simple components. Over the course of the essay, it becomes clear that the manufacturers of the chainsaws, which loggers use to cut down cedar trees in the Pacific Northwest, have just as much of an impact as the mining unions wherever the graphite is sourced. Read exposes the massive web expanding from a basic pencil, illustrating that no one person is solely responsible for the creation of any commodity—not even one as common as a pencil used in every classroom and household nationwide.

As a free capitalist country, we let the market dictate the demand for goods, which allows people to build businesses around fulfilling that demand and setting a fair price. Why are we not doing the same with education?

We know that as a country, we demand and will continue to demand lumber, metal fabrication, road building and maintenance, and the transportation of goods. So why are we not training people to take care of those essential needs? This demand is not a secret. The American Society of Civil Engineers has stated that the nation's infrastructure—including roads, bridges, water systems, and electrical grids—has been underfunded and neglected for decades.* We can attribute many infrastructure problems to a lack of skilled workers available to perform necessary maintenance and upgrades.

Despite some exposure to global political and economic history in high school classes, students in the US can't fathom the true needs of our country. Without the benefit of context, none of the aforementioned red flags registered with me as a young student. No, I was doing exactly what I had been coached to do. I put my nose to the academic grindstone and somehow got into a mediocre, albeit expensive, state university. In my heart, I believed that if I just stayed the course, I'd make enough money that I wouldn't have to worry about the writing on the wall. I figured if I could just graduate from

---

* James McBride, Noah Berman, and Anshu Siripurapu, "The State of US Infrastructure," Council on Foreign Relations, updated September 20, 2023, https://www.cfr.org/backgrounder/state-us-infrastructure.

college, there would be no need for me to learn any practical trade skills.

Yes, I, the generally educated American student, could pay someone to come and fix my sink, solve my electrical issues, or repair my car. My time, I was told, would be more valuable dedicated to whatever corporation enticed me to come work for it upon graduation. Even as I signed the high-interest loan papers as an eighteen-year-old kid, I failed to see the cracks in the educational obelisk, and I remained naively optimistic for the future.

4

BLIND OPTIMISM

MY JOURNEY THROUGH THE EDUCATION TRAP

HONESTLY CANNOT RECALL ANY PARTICU-lar class or professor that made a big impact on my life. Once I got to college, things seemed very trans-actional. I met with my advisor every semester to see which courses I needed to check off my prede-termined list, and I chose whatever seemed interest-ing. Of course, some of the classes held my interest around history and statecraft, but many courses were fillers to complete my general education require-ments. I recall courses about world rhythms, running a marathon, and the theory of death. These courses were not bad, per se, but looking back through an objective lens, I can see that none of them prepared me to be an adaptable and well-rounded working citizen, and each one came with a hefty price tag.

As my four-year coursework came to a close, I was still blindly optimistic that all the time I'd spent going through the motions would lead to that well-paying job I'd been promised. However, as I approached my final semesters, many of my soft leads in the job market didn't pan out because of economic conditions. Like many of my unskilled millennial brethren graduating college between 2008 and 2010, I entered an era of chaos for the new breed of digital knowledge worker.

In 2008, the Great Recession and housing crisis crippled our country. I remember sitting in my little college apartment studying for an exam on the history of Pakistani and Indian nuclear relations, when it dawned on me that something about the economy felt off. I also remember feeling a distinct lack of worry. Still, I believed I was studying *meaningful* things. I was getting a handle on world history through my political science degree (I use the word "science" loosely), and I knew, with no hard evidence, that some firm, corporation, or institute of higher education would be happy to pay me handsomely for that knowledge. Plus, every recession we'd ever been through never seemed to last long. *By the time I graduate*, I thought, *we will be through this and better than ever.*

Real Gross Domestic Product

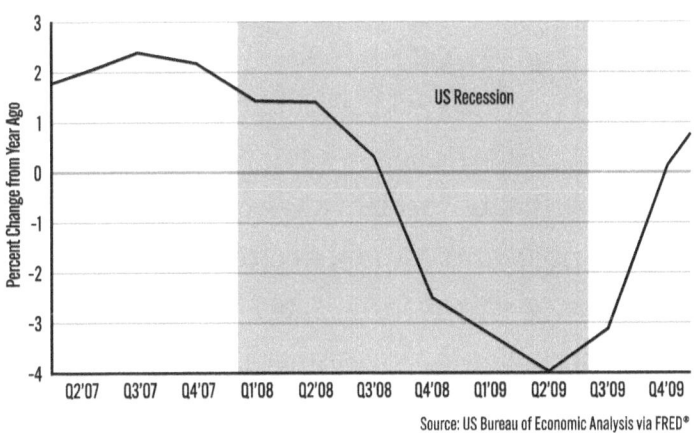

Source: US Bureau of Economic Analysis via FRED®

Of course, hindsight is twenty-twenty, and now, knowing how the economic crisis played out, I would've made drastically different decisions. Instead, I stuck to the party line, even after graduation. I applied for hundreds of entry-level jobs across nearly every industry, and I received zero offers. Instead of freaking out and realizing I was one of millions of American graduates with a useless piece of paper and a head full of trivia, I experienced a different phenomenon, one that, ironically, I had never studied during my *general* education: cognitive dissonance.

COGNITIVE DISSONANCE

In the early 1950s, a psychologist by the name of Leon Festinger was stumped. He couldn't understand why large groups of people who held strong beliefs could continue to hold on to them when presented with factual information that countered those exact beliefs. This phenomenon had repeated itself throughout history, including in Nazi Germany.

Festinger defined cognitive dissonance as psychological discomfort or tension that arises when an individual holds two or more contradictory beliefs, values, or attitudes, especially when their behavior conflicts with their beliefs.* In order to gain a real-

---

*   Read more about Festinger and cognitive dissonance in an article by Zawn Villines, "What Is Cognitive Dissonance?,"...

life understanding of people with cognitive dissonance, he decided to infiltrate a doomsday cult to
study it directly. Posing as a believer, he spent time
developing relationships with members as they
eagerly awaited the date their leader had preached
would end the world with a flood. Yet as time went on
and the date came and went with no rising water, he
observed something interesting. The members, presented with the fact that their leader's prophecy had
been false, actually doubled down on their belief.

Festinger and his colleagues noted that in order
to deal with the discomfort of being wrong, the cult
members partook in mental gymnastics to find any
means to justify their original beliefs. Most of the
members shook off the bad prophecy like a duck
shedding water from its back. They dug in their heels
and offered arguments to strengthen, not weaken,
their original commitment. But why?

Festinger argued that when humans are presented with information that counters a long-held

---

...*Medical News Today*, updated January 15, 2024, https://www.
medicalnewstoday.com/articles/326738.

belief, we experience an emotional "drag." The brain naturally reduces uplifting neurotransmitters during the mental struggle, which often leads to depression—especially if we have invested significant sums of money and time into the belief. The only way to alleviate this chain of emotional discomfort is through hits of a magic brain juice known as dopamine and serotonin. And what better way to get a quick shot of that juice than firing off a couple of mental confirmations? Specifically, we might think, *Maybe I am right* or *There is no way I was wrong!*

I found myself engaging in exactly those mental gymnastics after my undergraduate graduation. I hadn't joined a death cult, of course, but my fellow graduates and I had encountered blatant evidence that contradicted everything we'd been told would happen when we finished school. Our prophetic date of guaranteed success after college had come and gone, and most of us were left shell-shocked and scrambling for dopamine hits as we desperately tried to convince ourselves that the pile of debt we'd accrued *was worth it* and that the litany of knowledge we had studied was valuable. Like my "cult" brethren, my cognitive dissonance was running full bore in my barely formed prefrontal cortex, and I did what believers do best—I doubled down.

Even though I saw others struggling in the same way I was, I was also extremely stubborn—making me even more prone to cognitive dissonance. If those I trusted said this path should work, by God, I was going to make it work. That deep-rooted genetic hardheadedness would prove to be one of the few things that helped me cope with my newly forming worldview. Plus, my great-grandparents and family had stowed away on ships from Greece in the early 1900s, had fought in both world wars, and had taken advantage of the Smith–Hughes Act to learn a trade to support their family for generations. Though the target had changed, we had a history of following the American dream and seeing it pay off. So, who was I to go against that trend? I knew the course I was on and what the output was supposed to be. Despite the economic circumstances I faced upon college graduation, I felt that knowledge work was the new social currency. Despite the negative signs, I believed it was time to extend my search for work, turn over every single stone I encountered, and find out the real street value of my expensive piece of paper.

The market was saturated with clones just like me, and the differentiators in getting a paid gig came down to who you knew or what school you had gone to. Unfortunately for me, my family held zero connections and my undergraduate school was average at best. But what I did have was that aforementioned generational stubbornness.

After shopping my skills around everywhere imaginable in the US with zero luck, I decided to pimp out my general education overseas. What followed was a series of unpaid internships in various countries. My logic went that if I could just add international real-world experience to my tiny résumé, the companies that had denied me right out of school would not be able to say no when I reapplied.

I drained my piggy bank to support nearly two years of foreign stints in the Republic of Georgia, Kyrgyzstan, and Austria, but when it came time to apply once more for jobs in the corporate world, I was again met with rejection. At this point, I had people in my corner starting to plant the bug in my ear that maybe it was time to consider trade work, or at least learn a skill to support myself while I kept up my search. But no, instead I turned up the dial on my cognitive dissonance to one hundred and concluded that it was not my lack of any discernable skill holding me back from living out that promised American dream. No, no. It must be because I didn't have *enough* education. With those impressive mental gymnastics, I did two backflips off the high bar and stuck the landing, deciding that the answer to my problems lay in my lack of a *master's* degree.

GRADUATE SCHOOL

Thankfully, my subconscious doubts about the true value of knowledge work had already taken root deep in the recesses of my brain, and I felt that taking on more debt for *more* higher education was probably fraught with peril. So, instead of applying to American graduate universities that cost hundreds of thousands of dollars, I once again looked outside the borders of our country for a solution. It turned out that two countries would subsidize higher education for international students: Finland and Saudi Arabia.

Considering that I had already spent time in northern Europe, I figured I'd give the desert a go, and I soon found myself boarding a flight in Amman, Jordan, with a one-way ticket to the Kingdom of Saudi Arabia. It turned out learning Arabic and living in the deserts of Saudi Arabia for a free education was the only way I could accommodate my waning cognitive dissonance on education being the answer to long-term success. You'd think that attending class in a thobe* and eating halal food every day in 120-degree heat would be an obvious clue that I had somehow gotten off track in working toward my own *American* dream, but you'd be wrong.

After a few semesters of what turned out to be a high-quality general business education, the fact that I was the only non-Muslim, openly Christian American student caught up with me. The Arab Spring had begun, and revolts erupted all over the Middle East. Though Saudi Arabia was relatively calm,

---

*   Saudi traditional dress

the Muslim student base was diverse, and the mostly hollow death threats started to accumulate. When my professors had to wipe away "Death to all Americans" from the whiteboard every time I entered a classroom, I decided to heed the American consulate general's advice and head home.

With only a partially completed degree in hand, I was once again living in my parents' basement and trying to figure out how to make things work. What followed was a precision attack on the workforce, with my new résumé that touted—and completely exaggerated—my new international experience. I applied for thousands of entry-level jobs while once again making the harebrained decision to take on more debt to finish the degree I had started in the KSA.

ENTRY LEVEL

With my long Lawrence of Arabia beard shaved off, I knew I had to make some moves. It had been close to six years since I started my journey through higher education, and I had nothing to show for it beyond a college degree and a few unpaid internships. So, in what I saw as a final Hail Mary, I applied to top-tier universities to see if I could get my stubborn foot in the door and finish my half-completed master's degree from Saudi Arabia. I was shocked to get a few nibbles, and in short order, I found myself finalizing the loan paperwork to finish my master's at Johns Hopkins University.

The months leading up to my start date at Johns Hopkins saw me spending all hours of the day in my parents' basement, applying for jobs around the world with the hope of working in a meaningful role while finishing my degree. Even with all my newly acquired international experience and diverse education, it seemed impossible to break through. I got short-listed or strung along by companies but rarely made it to the interview stage. This song and dance went on for about a year, and I soon found myself wrapping up my final semester at Johns Hopkins. It was in this sixth year of university study that I had a breakthrough.

IBM had a posting for a management consulting job that I was completely unqualified for. In an attempt to try something different and to set myself apart from other candidates, I did a little digging on social media and found the hiring manager's information. I sent an open email pleading my case for employment. The manager called me. I believe my desperation, masked as overt enthusiasm, struck a chord with him, and he vowed to put me at the top of the list of candidates. For a moment, I was ecstatic, but then he broke the news: He said the requisition was open, but like most companies at the time, there was an indefinite hiring freeze.

Devastated once again, I vowed to keep in contact with this team to show my eagerness. When the hiring freeze was lifted, I wanted to be their *only* choice. For the next eight months, I led a campaign of self-education on IBM's position in the market, which I shared with the hiring manager on a biweekly basis. Like clockwork, I sent a short but informative email on everything I had learned in the space of disaster recovery management consulting. My emails were like a brief on current affairs that (hopefully) pertained to the manager's daily work. Every time I sent one of these emails, I'd receive a response saying, "This is amazing, thank you. PS: req still on hold." And every time, I would die a little inside.

Then, right as I was finalizing my graduation from Johns Hopkins and anticipating the need to start paying back my newest student loans, it happened. The email I'd been waiting for since leaving high school six years earlier came through—a job offer.

When I double-clicked on the PDF, my elation was soon met with the reality of what an entry-level job as a digital knowledge worker had turned into. Six years of school, international jockeying, loads of debt, and a desire to pursue the American dream had brought me to this moment, and the number on the screen astounded me.

It wasn't the six-figure salary I'd built up in my head. Instead, it netted out right around $50,000. Now, don't get me wrong. I was excited to have an offer, but I immediately thought of two guys I still kept in touch with from high school. They had both gone into the trades and had been making close to $75,000 per year—for the past *six* years—all while I paid to toil away in universities. After I did the math, I realized my salary would allow us to save only about a hundred dollars a month after rent, gas, and the monthly payment on my student loan.

It was in that moment looking at an offer letter from one of the biggest corporations in the world that my cognitive dissonance finally faltered. I had stuck with the prescribed path despite all the warning signs, doubled down on general higher education, and sought the dream my family had for me—and lo and behold, it was a sham.

My prophets had lied to me, and frankly, I was pissed.

DEATH OF THE
GOLDEN-WATCH ERA

"It wasn't for me," my grandfather said with a chuckle as he recounted the circumstances around his retirement in 1991. "Once my company was being restructured, they brought in a bunch of Ivy Leaguers, many who hadn't even visited the guys in the field. I had several meetings with them but ultimately chose to take the early retirement package, and I think that was the right move."

At the ripe old age of eighty-eight, my grandfather Hans is the hardest worker I know. He's still out every day welding, driving nails, and finding manual projects to dig into to keep his mind sharp despite early signs of dementia. His father, Edgar, was a welder by trade and brought his kids up in a post-Depression Southern household. My grandfather and his brother kept horses, raised chickens, mended fences, and tended to gardens while remaining barefoot most of the year. If something broke around their South Georgia stomping grounds, they fixed it. That included cars, tractors, and any other piece of equipment that helped them make ends meet.

As my grandfather came of age in the post–World War II era, he had the benefit of a relatively peaceful time, with growing prosperity in America. He was also a benefactor of the Smith–Hughes Act. "I remember it being a focal point, especially for the boys," he said. "In junior high, they taught us about electrical currents and had us wiring up small projects. Once we got to high school, we could either choose metal shop or woodshop," he continued. "For all four years, we learned the basics of craftsmanship and how to build stuff with our hands. I think at the time, even though college was becoming more prevalent, it was just expected that you could build and maintain things once you left school."

As he neared graduation, he had the option to go into the trades or to attend college. Because he was a good student, his counselor had advised him to go to a four-year university, but that was out of reach financially for my grandfather's family. Instead, he settled for a two-year college where he earned an associate's degree in engineering, which ran him a cool four hundred dollars per year. He remembered the coursework being heavily focused on math, drafting, electricity, and other more technical courses that pertained to the needs of the field at the time.

"When I graduated from college in 1959, I had a few interviews that were set up through the school," he said. "One I remember was a power plant out in Texas, but the noise there was too loud, and I knew I didn't want to spend the rest of my life listening to it, so I wrote that one off. The second was the Blue Bird Corporation, a company closer to home that was building school buses, and I thought, well, that would be pretty cool."

Given his mechanical background, my grandfather settled into a junior role working with fleet vehicles. "You know, I could've seen myself retiring from there, and that's actually the mentality I had going in. Back then, when you picked a company to work for, the mindset was that you'd be there for the next thirty years." However, after a two-year stint working on buses, an opportunity came through a friend to interview at one of the larger companies in the state, Georgia Power. With a little encouragement, he attended the interview and was offered a job with significantly more pay to manage the fleet vehicles for the growing company.

My grandfather took that job and did what he did best, which was spending time in the field, working directly with all the mechanics he now oversaw. He'd travel from shop to shop across the state and build relationships, and he was always ready to get as hands-on as he could with the mechanics. If they were elbow-deep in grease, so was he, which helped him build a reputation as a manager who wasn't just a soft-palmed pencil pusher.

At the same time that he was getting his career off the ground, my grandfather also became chummy with his neighbor who happened to be an electrician.

Every day after work, my grandfather would come home and apprentice with this man, for no pay, in order to learn how to run electricity and wire up residential homes. "Frankly, I just had a curiosity," my granddad told me. "While I was at college, I learned the basics of electricity but never had any hands-on experience. I learned more working with my neighbor than I ever did in a classroom. It helped bring to life all of the things I had studied. Plus, I figured if anything ever went wrong with my day job, I would have a skill to fall back on to pay the bills."

But positive circumstances at work eventually forced him to pull back on his electrical side hustle, because as Georgia Power grew to cover more and more of the state, so did my grandfather's role. His reputation as a hands-on leader preceded him, and when it came time for promotions, his name was always at the top of the list. Eventually, he found himself as the manager of fleet operations in the 1980s, with a secretary and a big office in Georgia Power's downtown high-rise building. "You know, I never thought too much about it. For me it was a job, and one I worked hard at, but whenever I had the chance, even as my responsibilities increased, I wanted to spend time out in the field, and I did that as much as I could."

When I asked him about the culture of the company and how its leaders treated employees over the years, he said, "You know, they really treated us well. We had regular company parties and get-togethers, and they paid us fair wages. I was proud to work there and had no problems working late or into weekends as it was needed. I really enjoyed the work."

At his thirty-year mark in the late 1980s, he was presented with a token of gratitude for his long-time contributions to the company: a beautiful Rolex watch. Inscribed on the back were his name and years of service to the company. "I remember it being a pretty big deal," he said. "They had a dinner party with folks from all over the state. There were speeches and toasts, and there was a general air of excitement and gratitude."

Right after he received the watch, at the age of fifty-five, Georgia Power went through a reorganization. Consultants were brought in, and there was a push to optimize different departments. As part of that optimization, the new parent company wanted to place its own employees in many roles, including the fleet managerial role. "I remember they were offering early retirement packages for some of us, and frankly, it wasn't too hard of a decision for me after meeting with some of their Ivy League consultants. I loved the job while I had it, but I was also young enough to enjoy doing things in retirement that I hadn't done for so long, like building houses, building furniture, learning new skills, and spending more time with my family."

Just like that, my grandfather coasted into retirement, after dedicating thirty years to a single company. Unbeknownst to him, he was at the tail end of the "golden watch" era he reflected on so fondly. "I see companies today like GE, IBM, and others, and all you hear about are layoffs," he said. "We, of course, had shareholders in my time, but we always put the employees first, and I always felt that the company had my best interests in mind. There was trust from the top down."

In our new era of digital knowledge work, the idea of staying at a company for even five years is considered a feat of endurance and luck. If you aren't being laid off for things outside your control, the only way to gain a substantial increase in pay is to switch companies on a regular cadence. Distrust of corporate American leadership is strong among employees, and even companies touted as the "best places to work" are not immune to volatile markets. There seems to be a race to the bottom as technology continually outpaces specialized knowledge work and layoffs are the norm. With no trade skills to fall back on, there is a growing pool of knowledge workers who simply can't find jobs.

If only I'd had the forethought to interview my grandad when I was wasting time and money in my early twenties, maybe I would have at least used my downtime to learn a skill or trade. Instead, I kept the blinders on for all the years leading up to that first lackluster job offer from IBM. I was now a dollar-store version of the Ivy League consultants my grandfather had been so turned off by during his last years of work.

5

THE HOLLOW GRIND

CREATING DIGITAL DUST

D ESPITE KNOWING THE GOLDEN ERA OF corporate work was over and that the educational system was a grift, I did the "right" thing. I stayed current on all my student loans and learned to play the newfangled corporate game. My eagerness and drive to make up for six unpaid years of education was at an all-time high. I learned the right things to say and how to position myself for promotions, and I was never afraid to explore new opportunities. Yet with each promotion and small bump in salary, I felt I was still falling behind. The interest payments on my loans and the nonstop inflation that never leveled out made my progression feel more like a fever dream, running away from a serial killer while stuck in quicksand.

To make matters worse, the actual work I had fought so hard to attain was mind-numbingly dull. My area of knowledge work was measured by my growing ability to regurgitate known facts on PowerPoint presentations that would be leveraged once or twice before the process had to start all over again. Most of the work revolved around performance management and positioning myself and my boss as valuable assets who delivered, as indicated by often nebulous measures of success. Our key performance indicators (KPIS) were made up, and the digital deliverables and benefits we claimed to provide to customers were always overstated and more grandiose than reality. Despite the ick I felt about being a management con sultant, I understood my situation to be the plight of the digital-era knowledge worker.

The more I talked with others who had graduated around the same time I did, the more I learned of friends and family who were still stuck in the pay-to-play education cycle or were still trying to find work. Everyone I worked with was thankful to have a job, but that meant our small circle of unskilled workers all had something to prove—it was cutthroat.

In my first knowledge-work role at IBM, I was so gung ho for validation that when I identified an inefficiency in some internal administrative process our team was beholden to, I decided to raise it all the way up the flagpole. The issue was so glaringly silly that I felt brazen enough to write a letter to the CEO with my suggestion on how to fix it. Before firing off an email with a PDF version of my "open letter" about the inefficiency, I sought the advice of some more senior technology consultants I worked with. Without exception, each of my jaded colleagues told me there was zero upside to sending the letter. If the CEO, Ginni Rometty, were to reply negatively, I would probably get fired. If she were to respond favorably, then it would likely shine a negative spotlight on our team, seeing as we were the perpetrators of the inefficiency.

Having a healthy level of risk-taking panache, I decided *what the hell* and hit send. For the next few weeks, I sweated bullets knowing that email was sitting in our very popular CEO's inbox. Just when I began to believe it had been read and deleted, I received a response from Ginni herself. The email stated that she appreciated my ideas and would send a team to Austin, Texas, to interview me and hear my thoughts.

For a young consultant, this was the ultimate home run. I had zero experience, was just learning the ropes, and somehow caught the positive attention of our CEO for "ideating," which was knowledge-workerspeak for the ultimate value add. Yet as I waited for the special meeting to materialize, I realized through a series of emails that my coordinators kept passing the ball to more and more subordinate employees. This chain reaction rolled on until the whole thing fizzled out, and nothing ever came of it.

The thing I remember most about that experience was the reaction from my coworkers. They had all been beaten down by the knowledge work system and fiercely defended whatever fiefdom they'd created. One of my senior consultant buddies, who drank a little too much at client sites, waxed poetic about how amazing it was being paid to "tug our clients around" and how we knew no more about their problems than they did. He then berated me for my email to Ginni, insisting it was a threat to our operation because at the end of the day, we were "paid to run in circles and keep up the racket." With a prideful chuckle, he topped it off with something that hit my ear wrong: "Plus, I don't have any real skills to fall back on."

I had been bright-eyed and bushy-tailed until that moment. Hearing that gross perspective was like seeing the wizard behind the curtain. I began to notice the eggshells that every knowledge worker around me walked on. None of us had the hands-on keyboard experience of the developers we supported, and we were always overstating our value and inserting ourselves in areas where we didn't belong. We spoke in buzzwords and promised to "circle back" whenever we found ourselves in unfamiliar territory.

With nothing ever materializing from the back-and-forth I had with our CEO, and the "I told you so" attitude I received from my colleagues in its wake, I decided to put my head down and go through the motions. I focused solely on trying to build the white-picket-fence lifestyle I had dreamt about since high school.

Week in and week out, for years, I was on planes to identical cities, eating at the same restaurants, staying at the same hotels to collect points, and coming back home for a few days to enjoy the spoils of my work—only to turn around and do it all again on Monday. Outside of the week-to-week travel grind, my anxiety fixated on quarterly performance reviews, where there was constant jockeying to prove my own worth by hyperinflating my digital achievements.

As the years went by, at every new company I joined, the story was the same. Very few people did meaningful work to move the needle, and the vast majority engaged in verbal judo to take credit where credit was not due. It was an exhausting, never-ending cycle that did *not* result in the hardest workers rising to the top—a cycle I discuss in detail in my best-selling book *Turning Feral*.

Despite the tug on my soul, the deep sense that this type of work was devoid of true meaning, I stuck with it. I played the game as best as I could, and I quickly rose in the ranks of several Fortune 500 companies.

Before I knew it, several years had passed and my titles had changed to accommodate the *senior* prefix. My salary continued to increase. I was finally able to pay off all my school debt and begin tucking away a little bit of savings. As I approached thirty, I felt for the first time in my life that I was starting to get ahead. All the sacrifice, stubbornness, and blind faith in our educational system had just needed time to cook. As that feeling of joy about *making it* settled in and my debts were cleared, I was finally able to participate in the consumerism narrative I'd grown up on—new cars, landscaping, new floors, an espresso machine, and a host of other *things* that made life easier. The irony was that no matter what I bought, I couldn't fix a single one of those items if they broke. Toilet leak? Call a guy. Need my oil changed? Call a guy. Fancy Google floodlights stop working? Call a guy.

The veneer of success I'd created and held on to for dear life was all I had. Under the surface, I knew I'd be *useless* if anything were to fall apart in the world. Although I wouldn't admit it aloud, I knew that if the grid went down or a natural disaster occurred and I had no more "guys to call," my family would likely die of starvation or thirst. I had spent years in school and had now "succeeded" in corporate America, but I had no clue how to be self-reliant. I wasn't responsible for any of the things that made my daily life possible.

Then one early morning before heading to the airport to hawk my nebulous digital skills once again, I stood in my high-ceilinged kitchen and took stock of what I had amassed. As I looked around, I realized everything was a middle-class lie. I had all the things I could never fix, a stagnant marriage, consumer debt, and no creativity at work—and the path I'd taken to get there involved shackling myself with ever more chains that made it hard to break free. I tamped down my ego and realized I had been a patsy the whole time. They'd gotten me. They'd gotten me good. But now my eyes were open, and my cognitive dissonance finally shattered—and I broke down.

I could see the cult mythology for what it really was: a manipulative con that had stolen years from my life. But what could I do? You can't just run away from a cult. There'd be consequences for that. No, you have to plan. You have to prepare for a smooth exit and covertly build your skills for a life on the "outside."

In that moment, I could somehow sense how fragile my situation was. In hindsight, I believe it was my own intuition speaking up from the quiet recesses of my brain, which made clear that the knowledge-work gravy train I had fought so hard to get on wouldn't run forever. I thought I'd bought an expensive ticket for a bullet train, and it had turned out to be an overcrowded cattle car instead, rolling along on unstable tracks with zero standards for safety. It was time for me to face the facts: I had been pigeonholed into a career that was built on a house of cards, and if I wanted to survive the long game, I needed to extract as much value as I could from the charade while being more like my grandfather and building real, tangible skills on the side.

6

THE SOCIETAL MYTH OF SUCCESS

O NCE I RECOGNIZED THE FRAGILITY OF digital knowledge work, I started to notice more examples of my generation being completely ill-equipped to handle even the most basic domestic tasks. My friends and colleagues frequently talked about needing the help of a professional tradesperson, but the wait time and cost were almost always prohibitive. Some of my craftier friends found that learning how to fix the problem on their own was the most viable and cost-effective move.

One of those friends had been building an accessory dwelling unit (ADU) for a new home office. When it came time to run the electrical for his eight-hundred-square-foot building, he got an electrician quote that ran close to $50,000 and had a multimonth waiting period. In disbelief, he decided to lean on the small amount of electrical education he'd received with his undergraduate engineering degree. He watched some YouTube videos and ultimately did the job himself for a fraction of the cost.

An acquaintance of mine was a classic car enthusiast who had bought a car that needed a lot of restoration, including new metal floors. As he had done on past restoration jobs, he sought to outsource much of the manual labor so that he could focus on the more vanity-style work such as picking out seats, fabric, and paint colors. After getting a few bids, though, it turned out that getting the metal floors replaced would cost him close to $30,000, which was way more than he had planned to put into the entire rebuild. He quickly realized that he could go to the local community college at night, learn to MIG weld, and do the job himself for a tenth of the price—so that's exactly what he did. As a bonus, he learned a new and valuable skill for future builds.

My first direct experience with the lack of available trade workers came at the expense of the wooden floors outside of my utility closet. While I was off doing my knowledge-worker song and dance, I was unaware that my water-heater drainpipe had been leaking, allowing water to pool for several days and causing the wood floors around it to bow at obscene angles. Terrified of water heaters and knowing I'd likely create a larger headache for myself if I tried to fix it solo, I resorted to calling a handyman service. They told me they could make it out in a week, and I would be looking at a minimum of two hundred bucks for service and parts. Unable to wait, I was forced to figure out a solution to the problem on my own.

With a little sleuthing, I found the part online for sixteen dollars and braved the replacement myself. I had the water heater fixed within twenty-four hours. It was the first time I'd ever fixed anything of signifi-cance in a house that I had owned and "maintained" for years, and I was pretty damn proud. My chest puffed out bigger after fixing that water heater than after any promotion I had ever received. It was so noticeable that my wife thought I might have received a bonus at work.

Putting my own first self-reliant win aside, I started to see evidence all around me that the "call a guy" era was becoming a less viable option for manual problem-solving. With only two tradespeople replacing every five who retired, every unskilled person's wallet began to feel the deficit of skilled workers.

Even pop culture started to catch on. Acting as a great barometer of public perception, pop culture can be a window into what a nation is collectively thinking. Since the 1970s, the collective perception of trade work had been turning lukewarm at best. For example, in a popular 1974 song by musician Charlie Daniels, he belted out that "a rich man goes to college, and a poor man goes to work."*

That trope of trade work being honest but "less than" has held true in the public domain for decades, with blue-collar workers depicted as undesirable

---

* "Long Haired Country Boy," track 2 on *Fire on the Mountain* by Charlie Daniels Band, Kama Sutra Records, 1974.

across all manner of media. There wouldn't be a significant turning point and public recognition of the damage this perception caused until 2023 when, of all things, a *South Park* episode aired. Yes, *South Park*, the wildly successful and raunchy cartoon created by Trey Parker and Matt Stone, would offer the first real public outcry around the mistreatment and devaluation of tradespeople—and the creators did a great job.

In an episode entitled "Joining the Panderverse," one of the main characters, a knowledge worker, has an oven that quits working. After pretending as though he can fix it for a fraction of a second, he almost instantly opens an app on his phone that gets him in touch with a local handyman. The handyman promptly arrives, but the main character and his family are shocked when the trade worker says he's completely booked and it will be a month before he can fix their oven.

Coyly, they offer him an extra twenty dollars to bump them to the top of the list, only to be told that richer people in town are already offering him thousands more to attend to their problems first. What unfolds is comic genius, depicting a town full of knowledge workers slowly realizing that their comfort and way of life fully depend on the only two tradespeople in town. These trade workers rise to prominence as they are able to demand the high prices for their services, while the knowledge workers' jobs are simultaneously devalued at an equally alarming pace with the advent of artificial intelligence. Though it's satire, the underlying message of the episode is clear and resounding: No one knows how to fix their own stuff anymore, and we haven't educated enough tradespeople to handle the demand.

With the evidence mounting, I realized that my knowledge-working career would never provide me with the basic skills to survive if our system ever broke down. Though it may seem trivial, after fixing that water heater drainpipe, I began to seek out more domestic chores that I would've previously outsourced, and I tried to address them on my own. I intuited that I'd need to build a base of practical experience before I could ever consider breaking free from the knowledge-work matrix.

TED WILLIAMS

As a suburban kid growing up in the South, I found one traditionally blue-collar sport was practically a religion in our household: baseball. Every year that I can remember from my childhood was chock-full of T-ball and Little League games, and during the professional season, our TV was always tuned to the Atlanta Braves of the 1990s.

When we attended a professional sporting event, which was rare, it was in downtown Atlanta to watch my favorite player, Chipper Jones. Despite the fact that I was terrible at playing the game myself, it was fun to come of age during the steroid era of baseball. I got to enjoy time with my father and watch Herculean human beings like Mark McGwire crush hits beyond the outfield and into the stands with surprising consistency. During games, my dad would regale me with all sorts of stories and statistics about each player, which I would try my best to remember. And no matter who came up to bat, he would always compare them to baseball legend Ted Williams.

For my eighth or ninth birthday, my dad gave me *The Science of Hitting*, a book by Ted Willams himself, in which he broke down the fundamentals of batting: stance, grip, swing, and practice. Essentially, his thesis was that if you held the perfect stance and practiced *perfectly* for a long time, you could then study the elements of the game out of your control, like variability in the strike zone, and optimize your chances of always making contact with a pitch.

Ted was ahead of his time. He was suggesting the same thing Malcolm Gladwell proposed in his book *Outliers* a few decades later—namely that perfect practice is fundamental. That idea, however, flew in the face of what I was seeing in baseball games as a kid. Instead of a rigid, robotic approach, many great batters of the 1990s adopted odd stances or pre-swing rituals that seemed to go against Ted's fundamental advice. They would wind up their bats, swing their hips, spit chew, and still somehow manage to connect with the ball and send it into the stands. This phenomenon was a mystery to many people until someone did a slow-motion camera study of some of these "unorthodox" batters, like Ichiro Suzuki. The study found that within the last milliseconds of their at bat, right before making contact with the ball, almost every single player would snap back into the optimized and robotic form that Ted Williams had preached in his book.

These superhero batters had become so proficient at the core fundamentals that, over time, they were able to unleash their own creativity to make their pre-swing rituals unique and eye-catching. Of course, this was problematic for a kid like me trying to skip the fundamentals and swing my bat "like the pros." In my young head, I couldn't understand why my coaches yelled at me for trying to mimic these greats and then immediately pushed me back toward the fundamentals.

With stubbornness and a know-it-all attitude, I refused to listen, which unsurprisingly translated into my never becoming a good batter or baseball player. I skipped the fundamentals and tried to go straight to the big leagues, and the consequence was that I never made it far in the game. The kids who did stick to the "boring" fundamentals went on to see more success and maintained a love of the game, something that quickly faded for me.

Why relay this anecdote? For my generation, there is a direct correlation between the refusal to learn fundamentals and "pretending to be a pro."

Similar to my attempt to bat like Ichiro without the core fundamentals in place, so many folks in my generation never learned the fundamentals of self-reliance and basic sustenance. Unless you grew up in a rural area, had parents who camped, or participated in Girl Scouts or Boy Scouts, you likely never learned how to make a fire, filter water, or grow and gather your own food. As a suburban-raised kid, I certainly never learned these things. When I was cold, I turned on the central heat. If I needed "clean" filtered water, I poured it from a Brita water jug. And why would I need to hunt when the grocery store was a short drive away and always had fully stocked shelves? My fellow millennials and I didn't know it, but we were all missing out on the fundamental skills of life. When it came time for our first "at bat," the lack of education would show.

THE SHIFT

After my first morsel of success in replacing that drainpipe, I decided I would take over the lawn care, pressure-wash the siding, attempt to do minor plumbing, and cover other odds and ends around the house. I had begun to build a slow but steady confidence that I could do more with my hands than just change a light bulb.

I soon found myself dreading my weekly travel for work because it interfered with some of the hands-on investments I was making around the house. I planted a small garden, began frequenting Home Depot, and started to actually make things with my hands. All of this must have been a shock to my wife, who thought I was going through a quarter-life crisis—which was 100 percent true. At the time, I didn't have the refined ability to articulate my mindset, but it was a total crisis of identity. I felt in my bones that my career path had a finite lifespan, and I truly believed I had a lifetime's worth of hard skills to catch up on to have any sort of safety net when the bottom fell out of the knowledge economy.

I'd reached a weird crossroads. I was finally making forward progress in the knowledge-working career I had fought so hard to attain, yet I also found zero life-defining value or creativity in it. My personal life was also in shambles, which led to a divorce just as I was beginning to explore the world of self-sustainability. Unsure of where to go, I made a radical shift in my immediate post-divorce phase of life by taking on a fully remote digital role and moving to Atlanta, Idaho, one of the most remote road-accessible towns in the US.

I made this life-altering move with one foot in and one foot out of the modern world. While living in the literal middle of nowhere, I was able to continue in my knowledge-working career during regular office hours while simultaneously reclaiming a level of self-reliance and masculinity. In my mind, this move was the one opportunity I had to learn more than just domestic home skills. It was a chance to put myself in a position where I'd be forced to survive on my own. There were no big-box home improvement stores nearby and no handymen to call. When things broke, I would have to fix them. Suffice it to say, I had no idea what I was doing.

Just like my youth baseball days, I started by trying to mimic the pros with no fundamentals in place. Armed with YouTube and books, I did my best to imitate the likes of Kevin Estela or any number of the *Alone* series winners, but I struggled with their advanced approaches to survival and DIY upkeep. After some initial frustration, I recognized how truly deficient I was in so many areas. So I decided to slow my "do it all and do it all now" approach and instead adopt Ted Williams's philosophy: I would refocus on building a solid foundation for everything related to self-reliance.

Building from the bottom up, I began to think about the core needs for sustaining life. I realized that everything came down to food, water, and shelter. That is as basic as it can get. But the world I grew up in provided me with all three of those comforts through systems I had no exposure to or responsibility to maintain.

In his *New York Times* best-selling book *The Comfort Crisis*, Michael Easter analyzes the state of willing helplessness so many of us grew up in and lays out the origins of our modern predicament of being *too comfortable.* He discusses not only the historical context around how our ancestors made tools and technology to ease the physical burdens of finding food, water, and shelter but also how these developments kept evolving to a point where everything we do in the modern world is pretty easy—which is not a part of human nature.

People all but stopped doing physical labor and exercise, began to eat store-bought processed foods, and numbed the listlessness of modern work with pharmaceutical drugs. This detached, sedentary state has led to a crisis of identity across our nation, especially among men, where the knowledge of how to provide the most basic needs for oneself is lost. Despite my parents' best intentions, I too had fallen into this category of unprepared men. Although I was able to avoid the second-order effects of this national problem, like obesity and depression, I'd still never learned how to fix much of anything until well into my mid-twenties.

Ironically, one of the measures of modern comfort that Easter cites is the number of items in any given American household. The number of "things" per household is close to 100,000, and of those items, 10 to 30 percent are tools.*

Yes, in our modern comfort-laden world, where few people know how to fix things, it's somehow still the norm that when we buy or rent a home, we go to our local hardware store and outfit ourselves with a set of tools: a hammer, screwdrivers, pliers, plumber's and electrical tape, and so on. And we almost always place these items into some easily overlooked drawer, doomed to remain untouched. Statistically speaking, in almost every American household, there are enough tools to fix 90 percent of the problems that one may encounter. Yet in our comfort-driven world, instead of using these tools, we find it easier to pick up our phones, do a quick Google search for skilled tradespeople, and pay them to fix our problems for us.

As someone who had fallen into that trap for years, my move to the middle of nowhere was my

---

* Brett McKay, host, *The Art of Manliness*, podcast, episode 708, "Overcome the Comfort Crisis," Nov. 23, 2022, https://www.artofmanliness.com/health-fitness/health/podcast-708-overcoming-the-comfort-crisis/.

version of quitting the lazy habit cold turkey. Like a drug addict who must move to a new town to avoid seeing his old dealer, I knew I had to shake things up. If I wanted to build a solid base in craftsmanship, keep up with a shelter, provide myself with food, and learn the skills I had avoided for decades, I needed to do something drastic.

To an outsider, such red-pilling may have seemed abrupt. I'd left a failing marriage, moved to one of the most remote places in the lower forty-eight, and sought to figure out how to provide for the most basic needs of my own human survival. The reality, though, is that my transition into self-sustainability had been germinating for years. All those years in school, all the time seeking validation through knowledge work, and all the debt had seemed *off* to me, but it took me until my early thirties to realize I'd been learning the wrong things.

What transpired after moving to the woods was a multiyear journey during which I paid for the transgressions of not learning or prioritizing practical life skills. Between my corporate Zoom calls, I began to realize that in my new harsh environment, things tended to break more often than I was used to in my suburban past. Trailers broke, electrical boxes failed, circuits needed replacing, and generators needed maintenance. Propane lines leaked, tires popped, sinks got clogged or frozen, and septic tanks needed to be unburied. Freezers needed new coolant, new rooms needed to be built, and flooring needed replacing. And trees needed to be felled, lumped, and split into firewood to provide heat. I had forced a situation where my choice was to learn or suffer, and the acquisition of the essential skills came through literal blood, sweat, and tears.

7

THE COST OF TRADITION

IVING FAR AWAY FROM MODERN AMENI-
ties afforded me time to think critically about
the reasons for my lifelong lack of skill acquisition. Yes, the educational push for a knowledge-working career path had not been conducive to
acquiring valuable skills. No one had encouraged me
to use my own hands to fix things. But that didn't fully
explain how my cognitive dissonance had become so
deeply rooted.

I'd always felt like I had no time to do menial chores
around my old suburban home—not because it was

true but because I believed I needed to be "working" all the time. My prior measure of self-worth revolved around how long I sat at my laptop delivering some form of perceived digital value. At best, I would find enough time to cut the grass once a week, but I'd excuse myself from everything else—like landscaping, home repairs, and major remodels—and simply outsource it.

Reflecting back, the reality is that I did have time for all of those things. What got in my way was a concept that had been shoved down my generation's throat—the "time value of money." The best example of this concept is the classic story of a smooth-handed lawyer whose wife finally chides him into fixing their leaky toilet. With no handyman immediately available and his capability to fix things now in question, he brushes the dust off his stock toolbox from Home Depot and gets to work.

With YouTube open on his phone, he lies on the bathroom floor and initially makes some great progress, but at some point in the hours-long endeavor to reclaim his masculinity, the problem doesn't resolve itself and instead metastasizes. Defeated, he cuts off the water to the toilet, calls the handyman, and waits a few days until they can come and fix it.

When his wife asks him how it went, he gets defensive. He hides behind a knowledge-worker smokescreen and mumbles something about the time value of money. "Yes, honey. I *could* fix the problem," he says, oozing condescension. "But I've already wasted hours with no end in sight. At this point, given my hourly rate as a lawyer, it doesn't make economic sense for me to fix it myself." With that, he excuses himself from pushing through the learning curve and slinks back into the complacent comfort of a life in which he outsources his problems to other people.

Where did this idea of the "time value of money" (TVM) come from, and why has it become the de facto defense for knowledge workers who have lost any sense of self-sufficiency? To answer this question, let's climb into our time machine and head back to the early 1930s.

In his seminal work *The Theory of Interest*, economist Irving Fisher used interest rates as the baseline to explain how capital markets are balanced through supply and demand. As part of that work, he proposed the well-known idea that consumers and workers prefer a dollar today rather than a dollar tomorrow. Simple, right?

That book and its core concept set the stage for decades of theorizing. Economists massaged and molded Irving's original idea into the time value of money, which became a basis for the theory of *opportunity cost*. In the example of the lawyer, he was correct in suggesting that based on the theory of TVM, he shouldn't have even tried to fix his own toilet. If he makes five hundred bucks an hour doing his job, the time he'd spend to learn, shop, and then unsuccessfully fix his toilet *does* cost him more in unrealized income compared to just paying a skilled tradesperson to fix it correctly the first time, even if that tradesperson overcharges him.

Plus, is it really the lawyer's fault? The education system and economy he came up in touted the virtues of specialization, leading him on a slow march away from self-sufficiency. Specialization, we've been told, breeds speed, efficiency, and ultimately more productivity. With more productivity, we can keep the giant flywheel of the American economy going indefinitely. But at what cost?

If we think back to the early twentieth century, when the Smith–Hughes Act and Irving Fisher's economic work first appeared, it was a time when everyone in the nation needed to possess a broad set of skills to survive and maintain a home. Wealth and earning potential were lower at that time, but as the economy progressed and specialization and knowledge work came to prominence, there was a slow and subtle erosion of the common Renaissance man.

In those intervening decades, though, for every new university-produced knowledge worker, tradespeople were also training to accommodate the maintenance of everything the knowledge worker relied on. Until the early 1990s when society began to push trade work aside, a sense of equilibrium existed between the white-collar class with higher earning potential and the tradespeople who supported them. If a knowledge worker needed something fixed, they could call someone to solve the problem for a reasonable price. That balance reinforced the idea of TVM and planted the seed for a generation of knowledge workers who saw no benefit in learning practical skills. It would remain this way as long as the cost to pay someone else was lower than the value of the time they'd spend trying to do it themselves.

This perceived time value of money is at the root of our cultural shift away from gaining a broad domestic skill set in favor of digital professional advancement. But the fact remains that in order to sustain that economic principle of specialization, there must be workers available to do the "less desirable" and traditionally lower-wage work that the knowledge worker foregoes in pursuit of their career. Clearly, we ignored this fact as we began to remove trade education from schools during the late 1980s.

It's not hard to do the math. Out of the three million kids who graduated from high school when I did, in 2007, about 70 percent pursued specialized knowledge-working careers with TVM at the center of their ethos, and only around 10 percent went into trade work. Repeat that pattern year after year for a few decades, and of *course* we'll have an imbalance. We'll inevitably get to a point where there aren't enough workers doing manual work. It will become impossible to keep the idea of TVM—much less our country—afloat. When that equation plays out, as it's already begun to, that's when the dam will break and we'll start to see the mess we've willingly made.

The lawyer will be forced to try to fix his own toilet—not because he's eager to build skills outside of his chosen profession, but because his calls to a plumber go unanswered. Yes, knowledge workers at the upper echelon of earning potential may be able to ride out the storm longer than mid- and lower-income earners, but that situation too has an expiration date. When the small number of trade workers become flooded with requests, they'll eventually tend only to the highest bidder—the joy of basic supply and demand.

The story we are writing as a country today, in which we openly ignore the glaring lack of skilled tradespeople, is not new. An ignorance of harsh realities dates all the way back to Greek mythology. In the ancient city of Troy, the god Apollo happened to see the beautiful daughter of King Priam and Queen Hecuba while out on a walk. Her name was Cassandra, and in an attempt to gain her affection,

Apollo offered her the gift of prophecy in exchange for her love, which she readily accepted. Following the pattern of most Greek tragedies, after accepting the gift, Cassandra decided she no longer had an interest in Apollo and denied his continued advances. Doing what Greek gods did best, Apollo channeled his anger into a curse that he placed on Cassandra. The curse stated that despite the new gift of prophecy she now possessed, no one she told would believe her.

It's clear today that we need to not only encourage trade work as a worthy profession but also prioritize learning skills as individuals. However, just as he did with Cassandra, it's as if Apollo has cast a curse on us. We can't comprehend the gravity of our trade-gap situation. We don't believe it.

Perhaps a simpler explanation lies in a popular thought experiment about a frog in a boiling pot of water. As the water slowly heats up, the frog is unconcerned because he cannot foresee the inevitable devastating outcome—and does not know there's a steady flame under the steel pot. To the frog, the slow and gradual change in temperature is barely noticeable and mostly enjoyable, but once the water reaches a rolling boil, it's too late.

Most of us in the United States are still kicking back in a giant pot of slowly warming water. But what we're willfully ignoring is that without a huge cultural shift toward building well-rounded skill sets and supporting youth in pursuing the trades, we are on a path to societal decay.

To bring about true change, we must retire the concept of TVM, at least as a deciding factor in whether or not to take on a manual task. Instead, we must focus on a new metric: the "time value of experience" (TVE). The theory I am putting forward in our new world order is that learning a new skill or having an active experience in an unfamiliar manual domain is worth more than paying someone to take care of it in the future.

The mental shift we need to make on a national scale will require foregoing some of the economically sound math we all know and love. Yes, adopting the TVE model may cost more today, but we'll reap the payoff down the road.

As more of us begin to adopt TVE as a core principle in our daily decisions, we'll see a general leveling up of our national resilience. Given our current deficit of trade workers, the push for TVE will help unskilled knowledge workers gain vital and basic life skills that they would otherwise forego by adhering to the TVM way of thinking. This shift will encourage people to pursue work that is actually in demand—and spark them to possess proud conviction in whatever path they choose.

8

REBEL WITH A SKILL

THE MODERN TRADESPERSON

RUE CONVICTION IS SOMETHING THAT has always scared me—whether I encountered peers and family members expressing conviction in their religion or people who knew what they wanted to do for a living from a young age. For some reason, I'm just not wired that way. I was cursed instead with a gene that prompts me to question everything and forces me in the direction of general skepticism. Conviction, for me, has only come after much research and drawn-out internal deliberation.

In fact, I always thought people who held strong convictions from an early age were missing out on other life experiences. Perhaps because of the cultural ethos to "explore yourself" that was preached in school, I always felt bad for those who knew exactly what they wanted and went after it.

But hindsight is the best teacher. As an adult, I now look with a sense of awe at people who held strong conviction in their youth, especially the ones who achieved exactly what they set out to do. I now recognize that my attitude toward people like them stemmed merely from a fragile ego. *How can they possibly have it all figured out when I don't?* I wondered, my subconscious playing the question over and over on an endless loop.

One such example is a gentleman named Tom, whom I met in my men's Bible-study group. Tom is a fellow millennial, has two young children, and is doing exactly what he's wanted to do since childhood—construction. He once recounted to me that as a boy, he loved trucks and heavy equipment with an obscene passion. Although that's not out of the ordinary for a young boy, Tom told his parents he would one day work with trucks for a living, and without the slightest hint of sarcasm, he said to me, "That's exactly what I did."

Because Tom went against the grain of our time, he even experienced some hazing during his high school graduation. In the lead-up to receiving his diploma, the faculty had gathered all the seniors onstage and announced, one by one, every student who had been accepted into a four-year degree program. To make it even more dramatic, the school broadcast the event on a local news station for the rest of the townsfolk to be "in the know." Out of the six hundred or so graduates in Tom's class, close to 90 percent had plans to attend some sort of postsecondary school, while the other 10 percent, many of whom were going into the trades, were forced to sit through the announcements without recognition.

The irony, as Tom pointed out to me, was that he was never opposed to getting credentialed by a four-year university program. He just couldn't see the appeal, given his chosen career path. He knew he could start his company, make some money, and then go back to get his engineering degree without having to rack up a pile of unmanageable debt.

Young "high school" me could never have fathomed doing something like that. Leave high school, start a company, and *then* go back to school, if and when you need to, without having to take on debt? These modern-day counterculturists had it dialed in. Tom got his diploma and started an in-demand trade that sustained him and his family for decades, while I (and most of my classmates) spent years racking up debt and fighting over a finite set of knowledge-work jobs, clinging to the idea of TVM.

As an adult, I look at people who had conviction in their youth and think to myself, *Who was the idiot?* Inevitably, the answer is always me. Despite considering myself a contrarian thinker in many aspects of my life, for some reason, I couldn't see the forest for the trees when it came to my nationally prescribed education.

HAMMERED AND HEWN

Tom's is not the only story of a young high schooler who had the audacity to give the middle finger to the expected path of knowledge work. Riley Kirkpatrick was a rambunctious student more focused on athletics than his studies. In his sophomore year, he got into a few fights that were out of his control, and he ultimately found himself expelled from school. During that forced break, his mother encouraged him to find employment while he finished his coursework online. Out of necessity, Riley got a job in a fabrication shop, where he began to learn the intricacies of metalwork.

"I wasn't always the best employee, but I was always the hardest worker in the room," Riley quipped. "The shop was great, and I really fell in love with the work, but I was always irritated by guys who half-assed their jobs. The problem I had was that I wasn't afraid to tell them what I thought, which often landed me in trouble with the boss."

With his penchant for hard work and brutal honesty, Riley finished his high school degree online and set out for Missouri to attend horseshoeing school. "The circumstances in which I found myself in Missouri were pretty wild," he said. "I liked working with metal and loved horses, so on a whim, I decided that being a farrier may be a pretty good fit for me. Plus, I could largely work alone!"

At that school, he was first exposed to what would eventually become his full-time job, forging metal from nothing into something usable. "No longer was I held to the limitations of working metal in the fabrication shop, but I was learning tricks to form metal into anything I could imagine. The whole experience opened up a creativity portal that was like nothing I had ever experienced. If I could imagine it, I could make it."

As he began to build his business as a farrier, he realized he was pretty hard on his tools, which kept breaking. Without the extra funds to replace them, Riley decided he would use his newfound forging skills to make some tools of his own.

Over time, as Riley worked as a traveling farrier, people began to notice those handmade tools and ask where they came from. It wasn't long before people began asking him to make tools for them, which set Riley on the path of custom blacksmithing. "At one point, I couldn't keep up with orders, even after raising prices year over year. But with the extra capital I had earned, I was able to invest in more equipment and began to solely work on creative passion projects." Riley has since turned into one of the most successful bespoke metal forgers in the US, running his business, Kirkpatrick Forge, to produce beautiful axes, pans, and custom pieces that celebrities and other well-to-do people request months or even years in advance.

Riley hadn't expected the path he was on to be so lucrative. He acknowledged how lucky he was, in hindsight, to have had the rocky, nontraditional start he did. He credits his high school expulsion for saving him from a path of mediocrity and believes the education system would have sent him down a path that did not jibe with his personality or skill set, calling it a personification of trying to fit a square peg into a round hole.

TRIAL AND ERROR

"They have to learn a trade," said sixty-six-year-old Eric Dryden. "I wish it weren't true, but that's where the jobs are. Because we've spent decades demeaning and pushing the education of our youth down a skill-less road."

At well over six feet tall, with salt-and-pepper hair, the build of a man twice as young, sleeve tattoos, and a jiu-jitsu world championship title to his name, Eric tends to command attention when he speaks. Despite an intimidating physical appearance, the sincerity in Eric's eyes as he told me about his stance on the need for young people to pursue trade work conveyed that he meant every word he said.

Eric's concern did not come from a place of malice for knowledge workers either. It came from a lifetime of being mentored and working as an entrepreneur throughout different skilled trades. "When I was in school, it was all about memorization. That's what they focused on to prepare you for college," he said. "They weren't teaching us to balance checkbooks, to learn a trade, or any practical life skill. I saw early on that it wasn't for me, though—thanks in large part to a mentor."

Coming from a troubled home, Eric had learned the value of a dollar as he cut his teeth collecting bottles and selling them to his local liquor store to drum up enough cash for his mother and him to split a hamburger. Throughout high school, he learned that he could multiply his money by buying small items at local stores and then selling them door-to-door for double the price. It's that tenacity and drive that caught the eye of an older gentleman who decided to help Eric on his way. "This man knew that to be successful, you needed a few core things. First was discipline, which I had already built through my life circumstances. The others were communication skills, selling skills, and trade skills. So, back in the late '70s, he gave me a formula." That formula was key to Eric's success, and like Ted Williams, it helped him build an unshakeable base.

"The formula was simple," Eric said. "You go get a job at Sears and learn to talk to people about anything they need—be it paint supplies, home repair supplies, guns, tires, whatever. You do that for two years before you go and find a commission-only sales job for a few years. After that, you start something on your own." As Eric sat across from me explaining this simple formula, my first question was whether or not he had followed it. Enthusiastically, Eric replied with a smile, "To a T."

Unlike thousands of his high school classmates nationwide, who were on the cutting edge of the push toward seeking higher education for a knowledge-working career, Eric was one of the lucky ones. He had found a mentor who not only told him there were alternative paths but actually gave him a step-by-step guide to acquire the tangible skills he needed for success.

Eric went to work for Sears, then got an outside-sales job, and then ended up founding his own company in the janitorial and chemical supply space, which he ran for over thirty-one years, at one point raking in close to $29 million in sales per year. Eventually, he sold that company for a handsome sum before immediately diving back into another challenging skilled profession of owning and operating an asphalt company.

"What I see today is too much instant gratification," Eric said. "We want instant coffee, instant food, instant replies on social media, and ultimately instant money. We've taken out the struggle of life for many people," he continued. "If you want something you can't afford? Just charge it and take on high-interest debt. But those instantly gratifying things all come with a cost. Some of it is tangible, but some are a slow burn. Everyone wants the easiest path. College isn't necessarily easy, and it can be a great way to teach discipline to those who need it and can afford it, but ultimately, very few people are coming out of those institutions prepared for the jobs that are actually available."

In Eric's mind, our educational system is outdated. When I asked how we might fix it, and how we could help guide our youth down a more practical path, he grew a bit solemn. "Our educational system is one hundred years old," he said. "So is our infrastructure, and even our monetary system. No one is aiming to fix it, not on a holistic level at least. If we are going to help set our next generations up for success, we need to be teaching them things that matter in school. We need to build well-rounded and resilient kids—kids who can balance a checkbook and understand interest rates, kids who can turn a wrench just as well as they can recite Shakespeare."

PLAYIN' IN THE DIRT

Change often comes in unexpected ways, and if you are not prepared for it, it can crush you. For Chris

Young, that change came in the form of an abrupt end to a six-year career as a law enforcement officer. Unsure what to do next, he fell back on the one staple he had in his life, hard work. Chris grew up on a farm in southwest Idaho near the Owyhee Mountains. As a child, he spent most of his time on horseback running cattle and enjoying the outdoors with his dad and grandfather. At that young age, all he could ever imagine was being a cowboy, but as Chris vibrantly recalled, "My dad at one point pulled me aside, and we had a very real conversation. He told me that if I want to be a cowboy, the reality is I will likely never be able to pay my bills or retire. He told me I would work until I couldn't walk. And that stuck with me."

That tough conversation with his father pushed him away from a life of running cows, but the lessons he picked up along the way through helping his grandpa mend fences, take care of animals, and run big equipment left a lasting impression. "The one thing I remember was always loving the machine operations," Chris said. "I was running hay balers and front loaders ever since I was a kid."

So when Chris's law enforcement career came to an end, he made a hard pivot. Remembering his love for equipment operation, he went into business with his brother-in-law and started an excavation company, Dirt Brothers. "Though it was hard to leave law enforcement, I realized I had skills that were in demand," he recalls. "It took me a bit to get all of my certifications, but I had been around dirt-moving equipment my whole life. Frankly, the demand is extremely high too, so it only made sense."

Now, Chris and his brother-in-law are excelling in their excavation company, winning bids at regular intervals and doing bigger and bigger jobs. It's not surprising that although Chris didn't start out his professional career in the trades, his exposure and broad education in manual work as a kid not only provided for him in a time of need but also helped him design a new and more fruitful lifestyle for himself and his family when they needed it most.

These stories are becoming more and more common as we feel the pinch around digital work worldwide. Those who have a background in or early exposure to skilled work are at a distinct advantage when it comes to making any sort of dramatic change or life pivot. Those with basic skills, even if they don't hold a certification, are more likely to find themselves with work as the demand for skilled labor increases year over year. But it's not just those who have been exposed to hard work and skill development who are primed to take advantage of our changing economy. Those who see the writing on the wall, regardless of the digital profession they may find themselves in today, can also learn skills to prepare themselves for inevitable change, which is where the growing millennial "maker movement" comes in.

9

RISE OF THE MAKERS
CRAFTING A NEW CULTURAL IDENTITY

THE BEAUTIFUL THING ABOUT TRADE WORK and the skills you need to be more self-reliant is that you can learn it all at any age. You may not become a master craftsperson right away, or ever, but a little knowledge can take you a surprisingly long way. As I've gotten older and broken bread with people from my generation, one of the common denominators I've found is that our modern society has left us all wanting more.

It seems that one by one, people are waking up. They're realizing that the intellectual and career pursuits we were pushed into to provide the "white picket fence" lifestyle do not provide the most basic tenets of joy, satisfaction, and self-reliance. More and more knowledge workers are seeing that there is satisfaction in reclaiming independence and learning to make and fix things with our hands. The catalyst varies from person to person, but there is a slow and growing movement of knowledge-workers-turned-makers who are trading in their smooth-palmed careers, white picket fences, and antidepressants for a life that centers joy, self-reliance, and a sweaty brow.

Research bears this out. A 2025 study by Ipsos, a leading nonpartisan polling firm, surveyed a cohort of American teenagers along with their parents, teachers, and coaches to understand what career path they would most likely recommend or pursue after high school. The study was initially intended to gauge the likelihood that graduating teens would pursue military service, but the results showed a strong preference for vocational training, with 83 percent of respondents viewing that path favorably.*

---

*   Ipsos, "Half of Americans Would Recommend Military...

True, 71 percent of respondents still viewed four-year college favorably as well, but it's remarkable to see trade or vocational work coming out on top.

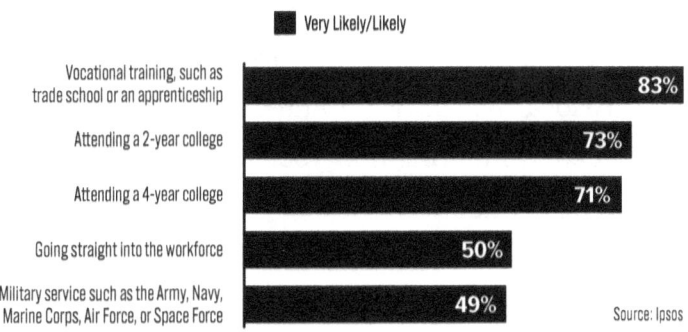

Americans More Likely to Recommend Vocational Training, College to Young People Over Military Service

Suppose your child/a young person asked for your advice about various post-high school options. How likely is it that you would recommend the following?

■ Very Likely/Likely

Vocational training, such as trade school or an apprenticeship	83%
Attending a 2-year college	73%
Attending a 4-year college	71%
Going straight into the workforce	50%
Military service such as the Army, Navy, Marine Corps, Air Force, or Space Force	49%

Source: Ipsos

While I understood how my own trajectory had taken shape, I wanted to understand why so many others of my generation felt the same way. Here's what a few of them had to say.

...Service to Young People They Know," Feb. 11, 2025, https://www.ipsos.com/en-us/half-americans-would-recommend-military-service-young-people-they-know.

A PRIMER FOR SOCIAL CONTENT

"Here I was at thirty years old, going back to what I learned from my dad as a twelve-year-old kid, and ironically, that little bit of manual training is what set me apart in the world of content creation." Those are words from a friend of mine, Nick Uhas. Nick fits the bill for a well-rounded savant. Grab a few drinks with him at a local bar, and I guarantee you'll be scratching your head, wondering how you could be so lazy and one-dimensional.

Nick was born in the early '80s outside of Cleveland, Ohio, to parents who were both high school educators. Nick's dad, before pursuing a degree and going into teaching, came up in a poor household with parents who worked a variety of trades: roofing, plumbing, hanging drywall—you name it, they probably did it. And although Nick's dad broke the mold by getting a "modern" education and leaving the trades, he still taught Nick the value of working with his hands any chance he got.

Nick recounted to me that as a young adult, he absolutely hated the manual labor his dad made him do. "All of my friends in our semi-suburban area spent their weekends on boats or hanging out with friends," Nick said. "Meanwhile, I was sweating copper pipes, nailing roof tiles, or doing something physical with my dad. At the time, I couldn't understand why we were doing these things, while my friends—whose parents were lawyers, technologists, or some other kind of specialized knowledge workers—were not!"

The irony, though, is that Nick's parents weren't pushing him into trade work. They wanted to raise a son who had a well-rounded skill set, but in Nick's words, "There was a full expectation in our household that I go to college. My parents had reinforced that desire by forcing me to do manual labor on week-ends, and I thought that if I went to college for biology, became a physician, then I would have a nice, cushy job where I didn't have to worry about manual labor."

After turning down a few wrestling scholarships, Nick did eventually find himself at a local four-year college to test the waters of higher education. It turned out that the required general education before even accessing the biology classes seemed stale and pointless to him. He knew what he wanted to study but was being prevented from pursuing it, all while still having to pay large sums of money for classes in unrelated fields. Frustrated, Nick left school after one year to pursue a wholly unrelated passion: stunt rollerblading.

The next decade saw Nick popping in and out of different universities during his professional rollerblading career before finding a way to marry his passion for biology with a budding interest in media creation. Yes, Nick was one of the early YouTube pioneers who cut his teeth doing backyard science experiments while filming them. At the time, he hadn't thought about YouTube as a career track, but it eventually outweighed any income he had made elsewhere. He quickly amassed millions of followers, which equated to sizable advertising revenue.

As time went on, however, more entrants came into the field as camera gear and editing software became more commoditized, which began to dilute the revenue share coming from the sellable ad pool. The ultimate irony here is that Nick was able to defend his margins in comparison to his competitors because of the base trade skills he had learned from his dad as a young kid. "I felt like I was playing the YouTube thing with cheat codes on," he said. "I had the ability to create things that no one else was able to create. Other YouTubers would have an idea and immediately wonder, *Who can I pay to do this?* Meanwhile, I had a garage with all the tools I needed, and the knowledge of engineering and construction floating around in my brain to actually make things happen."

This upper hand gave Nick an edge to continue down his path of YouTube stardom, but in his own words, "It's really a race to the bottom right now. What used to pull in $50K for a video, now some new entrant will do it for $30K, then $20K, and then $5K. Now the bar is permanently set lower, and as a creator, that $5K is worth more than $0, so you end up taking it." Seeing the writing on the wall, Nick took part of his YouTube nest egg and began to invest it back into where his family started: the trades.

"Honestly, it's an entrepreneur's dream," Nick said. "There are skills out there that cannot be outsourced. Literally, you can't outsource roofing or drywall to India or China. So, if I start a roofing company and make a certain amount of gross revenue, I know that next year it's not going to disappear to Malaysia, India, or Indonesia," he continued. "This gives me a security that I never felt while pursuing a specialized knowledge career that could be upended by technology or offshored at any moment. To me, this is a more long-term, secure pathway to success versus the specialized knowledge work that's pushed on our youth today."

Nick is a man with the ability to pivot and adjust to changing times, but that ability came from his parents' investment in him, ensuring he could work with his hands if he needed to. There was never a time when picking up a set of tools wasn't an option for Nick, and that broad skill set turned out to be the unexpected secret sauce to his success.

REMEMBERING TO CLIMB MOUNTAINS

"I never really thought of the trades as an option for a career," Nelson Dellis told me over a random Tuesday-night Zoom call. "I literally can't think of anyone from my graduating class that pursued the trades. It was something I was completely isolated from." This didn't surprise me. Nelson had attended one of the premier preparatory high schools in the United States and had spent his youth splitting his education between England and the US.

When Nelson and I met over a decade ago, it wasn't because he had evolved into what his other prep-school friends had—investment bankers, lawyers, and doctors. No, I had met and been drawn to Nelson because he was a champion memory athlete (yes, you read that correctly), and he had a knack for climbing the highest peaks around the world as a mountaineer—not exactly the "normal" path. So how did someone who had the ultimate grooming to go into knowledge work come to memorize decks of cards at the top of Mount Everest for a living?

Well, that answer lies in the path itself. Nelson had done exactly as his parents and educators had prescribed. He started out by attending a prestigious four-year university after leaving his private preparatory high school. It's there that the general education curriculum actually did its intended job by exposing Nelson to a variety of subjects, and it was a chance physics course that eventually piqued his interest. "I found a passion for it [physics]. I felt like studying this would give me the answers to the universe, which is what I believe most of us are looking for."

Nelson took that passion for physics to its knowledge-working conclusion by going on to earn a master's degree and then starting a doctoral program in the subject. It wasn't until he was some years into his PhD that he started looking at the other students around him and had his own cognitive dissonance shattered. "I remember seeing this one guy. He had been working on his PhD for close to seven years, just day in and day out studying the most miniscule thing, and for what? So his tiny sliver of work could be published and get tucked away on a shelf somewhere? I remember asking myself, *What are we doing here?*"

Eventually, Nelson got the courage to leave his program and steer his life in a completely different direction. It started with a hard pivot to computer science. He finished his master's degree in the subject and began teaching at a university, and he eventually landed a job in a growing tech company, WolframAlpha. Nelson recounted to me how he enjoyed the company culture as he was part of a skunkworks program whose sole purpose was to investigate difficult problems and explore the feasibility of answers.

At the same time, Nelson was also going through a personal struggle, watching his grandmother succumb to the initial onslaught of Alzheimer's. That troubling experience piqued Nelson's interest in studying the brain and how memory works. As he began his own personal skunkworks exploration into the power of memory, he found that he had a knack for certain memory exercises he had been practicing with his grandmother and began to enter into obscure memory competitions. In short order, he was picking up wins at national championships and eventually gained acceptance into the World Memory Championships, where he found himself at a crossroads.

"I had just started at WolframAlpha when I was invited to the World Memory Championships. I remember thinking hard about how I had always wanted to do something different and unique, and eventually gained the courage to ask for a two-month leave of absence to train for the event." Nelson would go on to place in the top ten in the championship, gain some name recognition, and cement his place on the main stage of memory athletes.

After the tournament, to his surprise, one of the main sponsors approached him to offer a brand ambassador deal and said they'd prefer to work with him over the reigning champion. "I remember them approaching me with a two-year deal that was the exact same amount of money I had been making at WolframAlpha. I honestly didn't think too much about it before saying yes. I knew I wanted out of the knowledge-worker cycle, and this was an opportunity for me to focus on getting better as a memory athlete."

Nelson went on to be a force in the memory athlete competitive circuit, which evolved into a full-time career. He became a corporate speaker, wrote best-selling books on memory, and revisited his love of teaching—all while continuing to climb the highest peaks in the world.

So what does any of this have to do with skilled work? Well, today Nelson lives in upstate New York with his wife and four children. Gone are the days of cramped apartments in big cities, as they have embraced home ownership and all the problems and opportunities that come with it. Nelson told me he recently had to replace his kitchen sink after realizing that contracting it out would be too expensive and the wait was longer than he could stand. "That was big; I was so proud of that," he beamed. "Before, a kitchen sink was just a thing that spewed water and collected water. As soon as I had to replace my own, it was no longer *just the faucet*. The intricacies that lay under there and the interconnectedness of all the parts and their dependencies on one another became an intellectually stimulating pursuit," he explained. "Plus, whenever I walk by it, I feel a sense of pride, and I see the result every day."

That sensation has now spurred Nelson to recognize that many of the things he had been coached to rely on tradespeople for could actually hold a deeper meaning. With some TVE investment, he could learn to do more of these chores himself. That relentless curiosity, the same thing that drove him into a deep study of physics, translates well into learning the basics of self-sufficiency and gives credence to the theory that difficult skilled work can be just as intellectually stimulating as puzzles, memory challenges, Dostoevsky novels, or mountaineering.

It's this same millennial maker mentality and slow realization around the benefits of skilled work that pushed me down the path of finding the right balance in my own life—one where I juggled my existing technology career alongside my new commitment to a pseudo-off-grid lifestyle.

10

THE TRUE COST OF IGNORANCE

IKE NICK UHAS AND NELSON DELLIS, I HAD found the power of learning practical skills much later in life, with an accompanying conviction that others should follow suit. The more I realized how little I knew, the more that conviction grew. This was exacerbated by my move away from civilization, where my suburban standard of "being handy"—which consisted of changing some light bulbs, fixing a few leaks with Teflon tape, and growing the odd vegetable or two—was put to the test.

In a few short years, I went through a self-reliance crucible, and it whupped me. I learned to run and maintain a chainsaw to cut trees for firewood. I learned to hunt and trap for both food and fur, and I educated myself on basic medical practices to help with the small-town EMS. I got certified in swift water rescue, plugged an ungodly number of flat tires, learned to run chains in the snow, became proficient at plumbing and electrical work, and the list goes on and on. Those first few years taught me that being self-sufficient was way more than having a few freeze-dried meals, a generator, and a water purifier on hand.

That crash course was supercharged when I ran for and was elected to a commissioner role with our local highway district. For two years, I put my knowledge-worker training to use for our small community by building spreadsheets and budgets, and I helped to source new highway equipment. Like my grandfather, though, I also used my time in office to learn from the doers themselves, and being friends with our little two-man road crew allowed for some extra privileges. As much as I could, I rode along with them to understand the intricacies of road grading, snow removal, rockslide clearing, and road oiling—daily concerns for our remote outpost. When our equipment broke, which it often did, our guys wouldn't hesitate to fix it. I watched as they welded new teeth onto our loader bucket, repaired trailers for rock removal, and maintained machines with laser-like precision. It was a weekly master class in understanding the amount of care and feeding it takes to run an operation that keeps just one tiny mountain town open and accessible year-round. It also cemented the idea that the journey toward self-sufficiency never ends.

After three years of pushing myself to learn as much as I could in the realm of practical life skills, I started to feel more innate confidence. I felt at ease knowing that no matter what situation cropped up in my life, I could find a way to handle it. What I didn't know, though, was that this budding confidence was about to be put to the ultimate test in two distinct and life-altering ways.

LIFE AND DEATH IN THE HIGH HILLS

It's often hard to justify doing something when you can't initially see how it will pay off. Whether it's investing in Bitcoin, planting a garden, or learning basic medical skills, you won't immediately see the fruits of those investments. Not until you trade that Bitcoin for fiat currency, eat your first cucumber, or help someone in a dire medical situation do you get to reap the rewards for your efforts. For me, all the medical and first aid training I had invested in paid off when I unexpectedly found myself cradling the bloodied head of my eight-months-pregnant second wife in my hands.

One day, my wife asked me if I had time to join her on a walk in the hilly woods, one of the many benefits we enjoyed living out in the middle of nowhere. With a thirty-minute gap on my Outlook calendar at noon, we set out with our two dogs for a short jaunt among the Douglas firs.

Holding hands and enjoying what felt like the first real day of spring in mid-May, we shared a kiss before my wife headed down the hill ahead of me. Just a hundred yards from our cabin, our two dogs—a 12-pound Maltese shih tzu and a 130-pound cane corso—started to get the "zoomies." Knowing that our larger dog was less than graceful on his feet, I braced myself for potential impact and yelled out for my wife to do the same.

Just as the words of caution escaped my mouth, the dog shot past me, making a beeline for my wife. The sound of my voice prompted her to turn and look in the wrong direction—toward the full-speed freight-train mass of dog headed right at her. Instead of dodging the oncoming collision, she stepped right into his path. He hit the brakes as best he could but ultimately took out both of my wife's legs with his dense body, right behind her knees.

The violent momentum of his impact sent my wife's very pregnant body head over feet, the back of her skull crashing hard into one of the many exposed rocks on our dirt road. The sickening sound of the impact reminded me of a .22-caliber rifle going off. I watched in horror as her entire body went limp and crumpled to the ground.

Moving through what felt like quicksand, I made my way to her lifeless body and noticed a pool of blood at the back of her head, just as I'd seen in so many movies. My shouts to her went unanswered, and having seen the violence with which she hit the rock, I was sure she was dead. As I knelt and held her bloody head in my hands, I had to make a quick and tough decision—I had to leave her to get help.

As I laid my wife's head back on the dirt, I thought of not only her but also our unborn child. I made the hundred-yard sprint back to our home, and grabbed my fire radio, something I was thankfully trained and proficient in using.

By the time I'd switched on my radio and contacted our county's emergency dispatch to get any available EMS units to our location, I was already halfway back down the hill to where I'd left my wife. From a distance, I was elated to see that in the less than two minutes that had passed, she had come to. It was only then, when I saw her sitting up, that I knew she wasn't dead.

Her symptoms were less encouraging. A quick examination indicated that her pupils were dilated, and as I asked her to recall what had happened, it was clear she was severely concussed. She wasn't sure why she was sitting in the dirt with blood on her shirt, and she wasn't even sure if she was pregnant.

Before I could finish my line of questioning, our small-town cavalry showed up. Our EMS crew, ambulance, and fire chief were upon us in what felt like less than five minutes. They'd later tell me that through the sheer panic they'd heard in my voice over the radio, they had known it wasn't a drill and that they needed to act quickly.

Once they arrived, I did my best to remove myself from the situation. Though it was hard for me, I wanted to let the skilled workers do their job and get her to the helipad for a Life Flight to the nearest hospital.

Within thirty minutes of the impact, on a beautiful, sunny day, we watched as a helicopter approached around our ten-thousand-foot granite-peak mountain and landed easily nearby. The flight crew made their way to our ambulance to begin assessing my wife, while I anxiously waited to see if I'd be allowed to fly out with her, thanks to ambiguous post-COVID rules. After an IV was set, I was approved to go with her, and we loaded up and went on our way.

Despite the harrowing circumstances, my wife was conscious, and we were able to somewhat enjoy the helicopter ride, twenty-three minutes of breathtaking scenery. The ride gave us both a new perspective on just how remote our home actually was. In every direction, there was nothing but wilderness, alpine lakes, and open space—the very things that had drawn us to our pseudo-off-grid lifestyle and forced us to start learning so many new skills.

Our time of reflection didn't last terribly long. As we crested the last mountain range, we could see the skyline of the growing metropolis below. We skirted the capitol building, buzzed downtown, and followed the highway before descending toward the roof of the regional trauma center.

After nine staples, three sutures, a lot of lidocaine, CT scans, and an extended stay in the obstetrics unit to ensure our baby was safe, we were able to leave and begin our road trip back into the hills. Through training and skill acquisition, we were able to handle a life-threatening experience with relative ease. I was immensely thankful. Unfortunately, I'd soon get another chance to test my skills.

MURPHY'S LAW

After my wife's accident, we returned to a state of equilibrium. I was back to balancing my skill acquisition with my knowledge-working career at a publicly traded company. I was still following all the "protocols" of suburban manifest destiny too. We had enough savings to last us six months, I maintained an up-to-date résumé, and I had alternate streams of income through book sales to ensure we were as financially "secure" as we could be. I truly felt I could ride this wave for the rest of my life. I was dipping my hand in the knowledge-worker cookie jar while living the life of a practical prepper and amateur tradesman.

What I didn't realize at the time of living such a purposeful double life was that our fickle economy didn't care about the stability of my family. What happened next was something I didn't see coming, and had I not cobbled together a well-rounded skill set of basic tradesmanship, we would have lost everything we had worked for.

SEVERANCE

Hot on the heels of our traumatic medical scare came another unexpected blow—something I'd avoided ever since I'd learned to eke out a fair living with a knowledge-working career: a layoff. It's not that I hadn't witnessed layoffs, because I definitely had. With the "golden watch" era of my grandfather long dead, layoffs seemed to be a seasonal treat that corporations doled out whenever shareholder value was in jeopardy after a bad quarter. Luckily for me, the niche I'd carved out for myself in artificial intelligence had always kept me at arm's length from the yearly onslaught that kicked more and more knowledge workers to the curb.

As with anything, though, at some point, your time is up. My visit from the corporate grim reaper came on a Wednesday afternoon in May. When a fifteen-minute phone call popped up on my calendar, with my boss and a representative from HR, I knew it could only mean one thing. Sure enough, the inevitable happened with minimal fanfare—along with 15 percent of the company, I was laid off.

To be honest, I wasn't worried at first. I had my little six-month nugget of savings built up, and I had developed a false sense of confidence in the marketability of my knowledge-working value. What I didn't realize, however, was that nearly every other tech company had just liquidated large swaths of their own knowledge-working talent, and the market was completely awash with overqualified—and equally desperate—candidates.

With only four weeks of severance pay, I quickly began looking for a new position. Despite the ferocity with which I sent my résumé into the ether, it seemed that every response led to a dead end. I would interview and see initial success, only to be told that the job had been closed due to economic issues. Something seemed off. My intuition told me that the knowledge-worker pool was bloated, and the culling of fat was permanent.

After an interview with the CEO of a data startup that had just been acquired by one of the biggest tech companies in the world, I asked him a pointed question about the number of applicants he had to comb through for the role. He was refreshingly direct, though not encouraging. "Oh man, it's insane right now," he said. "For this nontechnical product role alone, we've had over two thousand applicants, five hundred of which are extremely qualified. We were able to further cut that down based on those who didn't need a visa." He leaned in and looked me dead in the eye. "You're one of those people, but just so you know what you're up against, I have at least two candidates who were engineers at Google for the past decade."

At that point, the writing was on the wall for me. My educators of the past had not prepared me for the oversaturation of knowledge workers and the reality that we would one day be fighting tooth and nail for a shrinking number of jobs. The jobs we had all wanted no longer existed, at least not in the numbers we needed to support over 70 percent of high school and college graduates who pursued these careers that were allegedly "in demand."

Recognizing that gaining reemployment wouldn't be as simple or quick as I had hoped, I decided to double down on a few of the trades I had picked up over the prior several years—specifically, the ones I could likely make some money with. As the months ticked by, interviews came and went, and our savings began to dwindle, I went to work as an apprentice at a taxidermy shop. When I wasn't firing off job applications, I sat side by side with an artist who taught me the finer points of fleshing bear hides, mounting elk, cleaning skulls, and properly displaying turkey fans and spurs.

As I began to produce more part-time work in the taxidermy world, I realized that in order to make ends meet with our quickly depleting nest egg, I would need to find a full-time role. With winter approaching, we decided to take two paths to ensure we could make it. First, we liquidated some of our nonessential assets. There was no need for a second car payment, so as a family of four with yet another baby on the way, we went down to one vehicle. Second, I figured I would double down on another hard skill I had been slowly perfecting—trapping —to help keep the literal and figurative wolves at bay. With the winter months looming, I would help offset our income loss through the sale of marketable fur.

Thankfully, with the help of the hit television show *Yellowstone*, the fur market had seen a small rally due to buyers such as Stetson seeking beaver pelts to pump out cowboy hats for the yuppies flooding Western towns. With that trend in mind, I decided I would run a long line over the winter for all manner of fur-bearing critters. In addition, I was able to secure a contract with the Association of Fish & Wildlife Agencies to participate in a study on the live trapping of pine martens. It was an obscure study co-led by the University of Montana, but it paid me for my time in the woods and allowed me to finally utilize some of the scientific theory I'd learned during my graduate studies at Johns Hopkins.

Taxidermy and trapping, two skill-based trades I had only dabbled in during my self-reliance crucible, became our literal lifeline. Soon, our six months' worth of savings came to an end, and as I went into the trapping season, the economy was not showing any sign of turning around. Somehow, by the grace of God, I was able to use these side-of-desk skills I had been slowly honing and make a hard pivot from technology into trade work to help float our family for the winter months.

Fortunately for me, right as the trapping season ended and my last checks from the Association of Fish & Wildlife Agencies and the fur buyers had cleared, I received a job offer from yet another tech company, a whopping eleven months after I had been laid off.

I felt relieved—and immensely proud of myself for being able to scrape by with the amateur skills I'd learned. Yet the experience also opened my eyes to the true fragility of knowledge work. It showed that I wasn't immune to the economic swings or the growing saturation of the field, especially with the advancement of AI. It also made me realize that hands-on trade skills aren't just nice to have; they're a necessity in today's economy.

Without a few such skills to fall back on, I would've been hosed. We would've been forced to take on loads of consumer debt just to survive, which would have compounded the stress that we were already feeling. That stress played out in a brutal way for some of my teammates affected by the same layoff—with none of them having any skills in the trades to rely on.

They languished in front of their laptops as their depression mounted, hoping day after day that a recruiter would reach out to them. Though we rarely talk about it, the reality is that with no skills outside of creating digital dust, along with the ever-increasing national inflation, many people watched everything they had fought for get ripped away. Bank accounts went to zero, retirement funds were liquidated, and prescription drug use skyrocketed. For one ex-colleague, this unfortunate turn of events resulted in a suicide that left behind a wife and two young children.

The unexpected societal shock therapy made it clear that I needed to not just dabble in skill acquisition but learn a solid trade that I could do year-round, one that would hold long-term value in our shifting economy. Even though I was gainfully employed again, working for the *corporate man*, I decided that just like my grandfather learning to wire up houses after his day job, I too would learn a more marketable trade after hours. I once again invested in schooling, but this time it didn't require a house-sized loan and a lengthy application process. With a few emails and a check worth a single month's rent, I was off to night school at my local community college to become a certified welder.

11

THE NEW BALANCE

T WAS ALL FAMILIAR. THE CLASSROOM, THE eager students, and the air of excitement surrounding the unknown. Like I had done in my undergraduate and graduate coursework, I grabbed a seat at the front of the class, opened my notebook to the first page, and held my F-701 Zebra pen at the ready. Yet as I looked around the room, I noticed a much more visible stratification across the age spectrum than I was used to in past academic settings. There were a handful of doe-eyed eighteen-year-olds ready to start a career and a set of retirees looking to make extra income or support a budding hobby—and then there *we* were.

The aging millennials.

The thirtysomethings had come for a variety of reasons. Car hobbyists wanted to learn to install new floor panels, people were starting second or third careers, and folks like me wanted a taste of a more visceral, hands-on skill after nearly losing everything as knowledge workers.

Despite our different motivations, we had one thing in common: We were all there to weld.

Sitting in silence, waiting for our teacher to arrive, I clicked my pen with the same nervous energy I'd had during my first graduate course in Bayesian statistics at Johns Hopkins University over a decade earlier. At 5:59 p.m., we heard hurried footsteps and keys jangling down the long hallway of the community college we were huddled in. In short order, our teacher, Marty, busted into the drab, windowless classroom. Wasting no time, she grabbed her class list and started shouting out names. With fewer theatrics than I'd come to expect from my prior university professors, Marty skipped over the pleasantries and got right to business. "Okay, I need my TIG welders here, MIG welders there, and my stick welders in the back," she said. "Here are some sheets that show proper leg lengths for your welds, and how it should adhere to the parent material. If you came here for Metallurgy 101, those questions are gonna have to wait. We're here to get you welding, get you laying consistent beads, and make sure that you don't embarrass yourself out in the field. So, let's go over PPE and get into the lab."

With only enough time to jot down "Welding Course" and my teacher's name, I slammed shut my leather notebook, tossed it into my shiny new toolbox, and followed the rest of the class out into "the lab."

This was going to be different.

If you've never worked in a large fabrication shop of any kind, the first few minutes can be disorienting. The light from the LED bulbs on the high ceilings cast odd shadows on strange equipment, the sound of industrial fans humming at a low and constant decibel mute your perception, and the smell of oil and steel bring a distinct and odd sensation to the alien landscape.

As we gathered in a far corner of the facility by the grinders, our instructor began to shout over the noise, "Do not forget PPE, and do not touch anything with a lockbox on it! Now, listen up. I want each of you to grab a few pieces of quarter-inch steel scrap from this bucket." She pointed to a bucket near her feet. "I will be assigning each of you a booth. Once you're in your booth, familiarize yourself with your environment. I will come around to get each of you set up, and we will get you welding."

At that, we all dove for metal and weaved through the rows of welding booths, following our instructor like lost ducklings as she shoved us, one by one, into our preassigned booths. Mine was booth 16.

Inside each booth were the same things: a large metal table with a ventilation hood, two welding machines, gas lines, two power switches, and a variety of other welding odds and ends I had never seen before, all of which I had no clue how to operate.

I pulled out the equipment I had been instructed to bring with me and dumped it all onto my steel table: gloves, welding hood, welding cap, soapstone, chipping hammer, and a wire brush. As I organized the items on my table, I heard other students already striking arcs, and the still foreign but unmistakable hissing sound of metal being fused together.

Now, despite being a white-collar corporate desk jockey, this was not my first time around welders. In fact, the first time I'd been exposed to welding was twenty years earlier, when I got a job threading pipes in my dad's engineering shop at fifteen years old. At the time, my dad had cut me loose and put me at the mercy of the "shop guys," who were hell-bent on teaching me how to weld. In those formative weeks, I learned to strike an arc and lay a decent bead, and I felt rather satisfied that I could take on a task from an adult and add value to a shop that was paying me under the table.

However, as quickly as I had picked up the skill, I had become equally lackadaisical on safety, as most fifteen-year-olds tend to do. At some point during a temporary lapse of judgment and safety protocol, I had gotten my hand stuck between the industrial plug and the outlet. The result was my getting knocked out cold and sent to the hospital, gaining a new fear of electricity and welding that would last the rest of my life.

Given the anxiety of my painful history with electrical currents, I was more nervous than I expected about touching the welding equipment in class. So I didn't. Instead, I waited impatiently for my teacher to finally circle back to my booth. When she popped her head into my booth, she saw that I had done nothing and gave me no space for explanation. "What gives?" she asked. "Where are your electrodes?"

Sheepishly, I gave a shrug that told her everything she needed to know about me. With half an eye roll, she tapped me on the shoulder. "Come on," she said.

Picking every word with efficiency, Marty led me to the warming oven. "This is your working tool," she said. "It's 7018 quarter-inch steel covered in flux. That's what goes into your stinger. Ya know, the thing you hold when you weld?"

Dragging me back into my booth, Marty flipped on my electricity and turned on my Miller-brand welder. She showed me how to switch it to SMAW, the type of welding I had chosen, and set my amperage to 110 volts. Before flipping her welding hood over her eyes, she made sure my ground was attached to my table and that my steel pieces were lying flat on my workbench, and then she handed me the stinger with an electrode inserted at a ninety-degree angle.

"Let's start a weld," she said. "Tack those pieces together, and let's roll."

Sweating through my pure-cotton Wrangler shirt, I widened my stance and began to move my electrode closer to the metal. Looking through my auto-darkening hood, I did my best to aim the point toward my target and waited for the flash of the electrical arc to complete—one that I hoped would stay in the metal and not course through my body. As the electrical current completed and the spark lit my booth, my electrode immediately stuck to the metal, and my first "weld" was over as quick as it had started. Without a trace of sarcasm or criticism, Marty said, "Good, now we can really get rolling."

Before she had completed her sentence, she'd removed my electrode by hand and chose to guide me on my first run. Not unlike a professional version of Patrick Swayze at the pottery wheel in *Ghost*, she stood behind me and helped me strike another arc, showing me the basic motion and angle needed to pool the molten steel in the right way on the parent material. "I already forgot your name," Marty quipped, letting go mid-weld. "But keep doing this until you feel comfortable, and then we can fill in the gaps." And she was gone as fast as she had come.

At thirty-five years of age, with multiple degrees to my name, this was my first real experience with an educator who was out to teach something that our current generations have missed out on: practical, hands-on skills. This type of teaching, as a supplement to our more "traditional" schooling, is exactly what this country's students and adults need, and it's something that many societies, including our own, used to value. It's something that can actually spur creative and intellectual thought.

REVITALIZING THE RENAISSANCE MAN

Coming out of the Middle Ages, Europeans heavily populated large cities around the continent. As these cities grew, so did the thirst for broad knowledge. The expansion and growth accelerated with the invention of the printing press around 1440, when the first real democratization of information pushed humanity into what would later become known as the Renaissance.

Artists and free thinkers like Leonardo da Vinci, Galileo Galilei, and Niccolò Machiavelli produced their world-changing philosophical and scientific efforts during this time period. It was the birth of humanism as a concept, at a time when people were encouraged to study ancient texts and become as well-rounded as possible in as many fields of study as possible.

Perhaps not surprisingly, nearly all of the most famous creators from the Renaissance period began their intellectual pursuits in the trades. Apprenticeships were commonplace, and everyone started their quest for intellectual stimulation by first working with their hands. This foundation in the economic trade work of their time helped develop their intellectual curiosity and drove a cultural shift toward becoming as multifaceted as possible.

Just like Nick Uhas in our modern-day maker culture, the men of the Renaissance had an understanding of physical labor and material manipulation to give them a leg up in creating tools to augment budding philosophical thoughts in their brains. Without that foundation, many of the greats from this era might not have had the capacity to produce their greatest works.

That very quality of being well-rounded in vocational trades and intellectual pursuits is what gave rise to the term "Renaissance man." There was value in building a core understanding of the physical and intellectual worlds, which opened doors to eventually specializing in siloed occupations or pursuits, ultimately leading to some of the world's most iconic inventions, literature, and art.

In our culture today, centuries after the Renaissance, the term "Renaissance man" has gone through cycles of popularity. As noted in the history of our modern education, it seems we've placed emphasis on "specialization" over "generalization," which is largely due to the technological advances of our time that allow people to be far removed from providing for their own basic human necessities. Without the need to worry about water, food, shelter, or the tools and processes that provide those essentials, we are able to focus on primary educational pursuits at a much younger age.

In fact, the most recent pop-culture icon who touted the importance of being skilled across trades *and* intellectual pursuits was the protagonist from the hit TV show *MacGyver*. I remember watching reruns of the show with my grandmother and being captivated by the main character, who always found himself in dire, seemingly no-win situations. Yet no matter what was thrown at him, he always found a way out because he had knowledge about a little bit of everything.

MacGyver was the personification of a modern-day Renaissance man, and true to form, the writers made him a badass. Car broken down and no key to start it? No problem. MacGyver knew just enough about metallurgy and electricity to get that sucker started with a paper clip. Year after year, and show after show, MacGyver achieved amazing feats like building batteries out of coins and rubber mats or applying his knowledge of chemistry to create an impromptu electrolyzer. At one point, he even used a chocolate bar to slow down a deadly acid leak.

Though some of the scenarios were over the top, each one was well thought out by the writers to incorporate science and core mechanical knowledge. Without a varied and multifaceted education, Mac-Gyver would have been toast after the first episode.

Despite the success of the show, including a 2016 reboot, the appeal of the modern-day Renaissance man hasn't caught on. This is likely due to our education system's push for specialization and knowledge workers, as well as the overall ease of covering basic necessities.

Despite this resistance, the millennial-led maker movement is pushing the cart uphill toward a new Renaissance era—one where we once again hold well-rounded people in high regard! It's becoming in vogue to be that guy or gal who went through the education "process" and came out on the other end with practical skills.

During small talk on a Monday-morning team Zoom call, people are amazed to hear someone say they changed the oil in their own car or tilled dirt for their fall garden. Slack-jawed colleagues from surrounding generations are genuinely curious as to how anyone had the time, energy, or know-how to accomplish such a "magical feat."

My target readers know exactly what I'm talking about. You've likely been shocked to hear that someone with the same educational background as you had the audacity to learn practical skills on their own—and it's inspiring!

Post-pandemic, there is a growing trend of millennials and Gen Xers reexamining the world we came up in. Adults lied to us about what was important to study, about what was healthy to consume, and about consumer debt. Years and years of following the rules to achieve the promised "pot of gold" led to a simmering resentment over every single crisis and "once in a lifetime event" we lived through. Slowly, some Gen Xers and a majority of millennials and later generations are realizing that the education we were pushed toward is a quickly depreciating asset in a world where technology is outpacing Moore's Law by a significant margin.*

---

* Moore's Law is the observation that the number of transistors on an integrated circuit (IC) doubles every two years, with a minimal increase in cost.

THE NEW BLUEPRINT

In Michael Easter's book *The Comfort Crisis*, one of the key takeaways to combat our national complacency was to encourage readers to challenge themselves mentally and physically on a regular cadence. He calls this practice the *misogi*, which is derived from a Japanese practice of doing something mentally and physically challenging each year to foster growth and resilience. Easter challenges his readers to plan out something once a year that meets a few different criteria. First, due to its difficulty, the effort undertaken should only carry a fifty-fifty chance of successful completion. Second, it should be mostly about the journey, and you should engage in mindfulness during the execution. Lastly, the *misogi* is a tool for mental and physical growth. To achieve this, you must be open to change, and you must want to learn new things about yourself.

When it comes to knowledge workers learning a new trade or skill, I see it as no different than a trade-related *misogi*. The concept of TVM has conditioned us to ignore fixing the most basic things in our homes, so for those knowledge workers who want to expand their horizons and learn a basic domestic skill set, I suggest that you embrace the new ideal of TVE by pursuing monthly trade-related *misogis*.

Whether you are a lawyer, a doctor, an accountant, a code developer, or some other specialized knowledge worker, you have the same twelve months in the year and twenty-four hours in a day. It's time to dust off the tools you have tucked away in a drawer and challenge yourself to use them. It's time to fix or create something with your hands. My suggestion is that every month, you do something challenging that will help develop a domestic or trade skill that holds long-term TVE.

Each monthly trade *misogi* should be challenging and will require some prep work to ensure that you have the tools on hand to complete the task. If you are someone who has put off manual labor for years, I would start with the backlog of chores that have built up around your home or apartment. Leaky sink? Start by replacing that. Driveway needs to be pressure washed? Watch a YouTube video, head to your hardware store, and rent a pressure washer.

These monthly challenges should be hard, but reasonable to finish in a few hours. As you begin to stack wins on a monthly basis by changing your car oil, replacing baseboards, or soldering back together one of your child's toys, you will start to build a "fix it first" mindset. No longer will your knee-jerk reaction to something breaking be to call an expert or to replace the item altogether. You will begin to approach it as one of your monthly trade challenges.

On top of the monthly mini-challenges, consider pursuing a penultimate yearly test as well. Each year, pick a project that is not centered on just fixing but actually *creating*. As outlined in earlier chapters, there is intellectual stimulation to be found in hands-on skill development, and we should dedicate ourselves to at least one yearly challenge that pushes us beyond our comfort zone and into learning a new skill.

This yearly challenge should follow all the same criteria as Michael Easter's physical *misogis*, with an added emphasis on the outcome not being the goal. Have you always wanted to work with wood? Building some new deck furniture may be a great pursuit. Want to have a desirable backup skill in case the economy collapses? Take a night class in welding and build a meat smoker for your family to enjoy. Want to make your own clothes? Learn to sew or knit, and create something you or your children can wear.

Whatever you choose for your yearly challenge, it should be something you've been nervous or hesitant to try. It should be marginally overwhelming, and the desired output should be something you can physically hold—something that you could walk by, eat, or wear for months or years after the challenge is over.

12
CLOSING THE TRADE GAP

O
NE OF MY BIGGEST FRUSTRATIONS DURING
my knowledge-working career was answering the simplest question: "What do you do for
work?" Whether at dinner parties, at the gym,
on a plane, or when reconnecting with an old friend,
I'd always begin my answer with a long pause. It's not
that I didn't know what I did for work, but it was hard
to articulate much of what being a knowledge worker
entailed. I could've answered with my title, digital AI
product manager, but that only invited more questions. I could've said that I built out business require-
ments for complex algorithms that make decisions

on customer interactions to further fuel our obscene consumerism, but that sounds a bit too creepy. So I'd usually just laugh off the question and say, "Heck, I don't even really know what I do."

As I've matured through my personal trade *misogis* over the past few years, I have found myself answering the question a bit differently. I'm no longer afraid of stumbling over a response. Today, I am more apt to answer, "I work for a large tech company during the day, but I'm mostly a trapper, writer, and welder."

Though it doesn't yet yield the majority of my income, I've found more pride in the work that produces a physical product I can hold or that has provided income when I needed it most. My day jobs as a knowledge worker have always centered on digital dust, which only held value for a short time before disappearing into the void of some long-forgotten hard drive in the basement of a data center. Even the more visceral products I helped create that touched millions of customers in the digital world have all changed or been removed over the years. What I've contributed to the knowledge-working space has rarely had a physical manifestation, which is the main reason explaining my work was so difficult.

With trapping, though, I can slip on a pair of beaver-wool gloves every winter and remember the work that went into making them. I also have confidence in their longevity and the potential to pass them down to my kids and, with proper care, to their kids. And the books I write, a reflection of my own creativity, will survive for generations. My future grandkids may have the opportunity to flip through the pages and see their grandpa's handwritten notes. With welding, my family can use our smoker and think back on how I tacked together the metal to help deliver a delicious meal.

With trade skills, the output is always tangible, visceral, and real. They offer a direct line to cut through the hazy world of social media, nebulous knowledge-work jobs, and the feeling of uncertainty many of us have about relying on others to provide for our core needs.

Despite my transformation, though, I recognize that full-time trade work is not for everybody. For a balanced society, we still need playwrights, digital entrepreneurs, dancers, and accountants. However, I believe people can enrich those other job functions through exposure to and experience in hands-on skills, or at least by gaining a deeper understanding of the value of trade work.

We must value our ability to understand the world around us. We need to strengthen our capacity to contribute—to help keep things running. We've all witnessed the fickleness of our current economy. Those who can pivot, adjust, and develop a broad set of hard skills to draw on will have the advantage.

That pursuit to modernize the ethos of the Renaissance man is exactly why, at thirty-five years old, I was in a night-school welding booth at my local community college. Not only was it an investment in attaining a complex new skill to fulfill my yearly trade *misogi*, it also provided the security blanket of having an in-demand skill to fall back on if I were to lose my main source of income again.

That invaluable sense of confidence is what I wish for people all across our nation. We need to recognize that despite what we've been taught about specialized knowledge work and its perceived value, it is one-dimensional. When we focus solely on one pursuit, it opens up a risk vector that we inevitably overlook until it is too late. I was lucky. Had I not started exploring skills outside my "area of expertise," I would've lost everything I'd built for myself and my family—I would've lost the American dream.

Despite all the turbulence out there for modern working people, I am an optimist. I do not believe the American dream is dead. I just believe it's changing, and the rhetoric regarding how to attain that dream has not caught up to our new reality, with the unfortunate result of sending generations of students toward a dead end.

Students today need to understand that there are more options available to them to make a difference in our world and that it is no longer "college or bust." You don't have to be the person at a dinner party struggling to describe what you do for work. You can be the person who says, with confidence and pride, that you are a plumber, a welder, an electrician, a farmer, a butcher, or a mechanic. As more knowledge workers adopt the practices of this book by pursuing the time value of *experience* over the time value of *money*, the appreciation for trade jobs and their underlying skills will grow.

Thankfully, these ideas are beginning to percolate on a national level. The millennial maker movements, trade counterculturists, and even educational institutions are starting to catch on to the idea that without a massive shift in education, we'll end up in a tough and potentially irreversible spot.

A BRIGHT LIGHT IN A DARK ROOM

If you were to throw a dart blindly toward a map of the United States, there's a pretty good chance that if you threw it straight, you'd hit Oklahoma. Known as one of the "flyover states," Oklahoma sits in the southern central region of our country.

The terrain of this great state ranges from river deltas to plains to rugged mountains. If you drive across it from east to west, you'll feel like you are in a different state every couple of miles. This topography lends itself to a variety of different exports from hands-on agriculture, heavy-equipment manufacturing, and oil extraction. It is also a sportsman's paradise with ample hunting, fishing, and trapping opportunities that span all manner of game species.

This rugged environment has produced hardy people for centuries, and Oklahoma seems to export notably ethical people with a wide range of talents— including Will Rogers, Mickey Mantle, Reba McEntire, and Bill Hader. And with a hard-nosed work ethic as one of the state's unspoken core tenets, it makes sense that the National Wrestling Hall of Fame is located in Stillwater, Oklahoma, on the grounds of one of the state's main public universities.

With all of these blue-collar accolades, it's no surprise that Oklahoma has been a leader in vocational and trade education for more than a century. In fact, in 1908, Oklahoma was the first state to independently fund a vocational agricultural program. It was also one of the first states to accept federal funding from the Smith–Hughes Act in 1917 to expand that training statewide. Vocational training was the state's focus before and after World War II, with a landmark year for advancement in 1966. This is when Oklahoma voters approved a state constitutional amendment initiative titled State Question 434, which introduced new tax zones to fund the construction of technology centers across the state to help keep up with the educational needs of in-demand trade jobs.

In the decades following the amendment, technology centers were erected across the state under the banner of Oklahoma CareerTech. Just building the centers alone wasn't enough, however. Educators tied to the program began planning to ensure these centers could improve the future for the students of their state and ruminated on how they could do so in a sustainable way. They ultimately prioritized a focus on flexibility for students, which has turned out to be a key component in the continued success of these centers. At the inception, the founders built a framework called an Individual Career and Academic Plan (ICAP). As early as middle school, students can work with an advisor to plan how they will weave vocational training into their regular high school studies without giving one up for the other.

Today, Oklahoma CareerTech serves over 500,000 students per year across twenty-nine different technology centers, which equates to one technology center per school district. Here's what Brent Haken, state director of Oklahoma CareerTech, said on a podcast with Mike Rowe: "Oklahoma is unique in how we approach trades education. We really try to wrap around how you get exposed to careers, how you figure out which ones you are good at, and then we are going to train you so you are ready for a job as soon as you get out."[*]

Throughout the school year, students who opt in to the programs offered by Oklahoma CareerTech get bused to their local technology center at intervals and times that work for them—whether before school, after school, or even during school, depending on their individual goals. The trades and certifications that are offered also vary as widely as the student population. From preparing students for the local oil and pipelining industry by teaching polyfusion welding, to coaching students in nursing programs,

---

[*]   Mike Rowe, host, *The Way I Heard It*, podcast, episode 401, "Brent Haken—A Farmer Is Fixing It," MRW Productions, August 27, 2024, https://sites.libsyn.com/74011/401-a-farmer-is-fixing-it-with-brent-haken.

the options for an in-demand job at graduation are seemingly endless. Further, the programs coordinate with statewide higher education to help students not only gain the necessary certifications but also earn college credits in the event that they want to pursue a postsecondary degree to augment their hard-earned practical skills.

"We are going to teach you what the industry is actually doing, and many times it's actually the industry person doing the teaching. We aren't going to baby you like you may get in your regular class-room when you receive a bad grade," Haken said about facilitating grit and building well-rounded students. "Look, that kind of [soft] mentality is not gonna cut it on the jobsite. You are gonna get fired. It's about showing these kids reality, but then giving them support and teaching them to do things the right way."

Day in and day out during the school year, students across Oklahoma are hanging drywall, studying to get their CDL license, learning to insert an IV, running electrical wire, and apprenticing across nearly every trade imaginable. When asked how the program fosters discipline and hope in students who come from all walks of life, Haken responded, "It's hard, but it's not ever too late. You have to tie the 'What do you need?' to the 'What do you want?' To build hope in students, you show them how they can get there and then cultivate the reality of what it will take to get there. Further, these students need support on that journey, and that's what we provide, which helps them see the path to success—and, in turn, that builds a level of self-discipline."

From a young age, the students of Oklahoma's CareerTech program are being molded into well-rounded generalists. Upon graduating, they aren't required to pursue the trade that they trained in, although almost all of them do. For those who choose to pass on the immediate job opportunities at graduation and instead attend a two- or four-year degree program, they now have, at minimum, a skill that they can fall back on whenever they need to.

It's a model of education that embodies the true idea of what it means to be an American Renaissance man or woman. I believe we should adopt that model more widely to normalize *actual* general education—and lead the charge toward a broader nationwide destigmatization of trade work. However, for states that aren't as far along in offering support for these endeavors, there are tradespeople taking matters into their own hands.

In Dripping Springs, Texas, Briana Huhn is reshaping perceptions of trade skills through her own innovative educational programs. Her initiative, Huhney Bee Tools & Trades, bridges generational and cultural gaps, providing hands-on training for children as young as eight while also catering to adults seeking self-reliance and new career opportunities. Huhn's classes introduce participants to welding, carpentry, and other trades in an environment that emphasizes professionalism and respect for the craft. Rejecting the stigma that skilled trades are a fallback for the academically disinclined, she stresses their complexity and importance. "Engineering is part of skilled trades," she says. "If you don't have the people in production welding on the assembly lines, you don't have anybody making the products." Her approach encourages participants to see trade work not as "less than" but as essential, fulfilling, and deeply intelligent.

Huhn runs her programs in a way that reflects her commitment to authenticity. All classes are coed, which she believes is vital for breaking down gender biases early on. "If little boys don't see that little girls can do this from a young, impressionable age, then we're reinforcing the idea that skilled trades aren't for everyone," she explains. By teaching trades in a professional manner, even to younger students, Huhn instills both respect and confidence. "You're learning something that is potentially dangerous and something that could make you money for the rest of your life."

Her classes heavily emphasize practicality—students leave with tangible skills like welding, building furniture, and performing basic home repairs, as well as a newfound sense of independence. She told me about a young teenager in her program who had never been very hands-on. "I feel like such a man!" the teen said after completing his first carpentry project, which perfectly illustrates the transformational power of Huhn's teaching.

Through her efforts, she aims to inspire not just future tradespeople but also a cultural shift toward valuing practical knowledge. As she puts it, "There is something primal in us to build and create. Kids light up when they realize they can make something with their hands—it's powerful." By fostering that spark in her students, Huhn is laying the groundwork at a grassroots level for a generation that values self-reliance, collaboration, and the skilled trades as integral parts of our society's future.

ATLAS SHRUGGED

Whether statewide initiatives or grassroots efforts in a single garage, programs like Oklahoma CareerTech and Huhney Bee Tools & Trades build children up in a way that is vital for our country's longevity. Preparing everyone for an uncertain world by arming kids (and adults) with skills that have actual market value is the absolute best thing we can do. That preparation doesn't need to come at the expense of general academic education but instead can augment it. We need to be clear about our country's core necessities and the economics underpinning a limited number of knowledge-work jobs that are being further winnowed by AI.

In Ayn Rand's classic novel *Atlas Shrugged*, she depicts the ups and downs of a free economy. Industrialists and entrepreneurs push the world forward, but it's clear that *every* individual must contribute in order to avoid the stagnation and decay of society as a whole. There's no room for laziness. Everyone is expected to strive for excellence in whatever they do for the betterment of society.

Americans have long been known as a resilient, driven people who eagerly embrace new challenges. Today, that national identity is under threat. We can settle for comfort, or we can embrace that identity and become the bold, lifelong learners our forebears envisioned. That work begins with each of us mastering the fundamental skills of living offered by the trades. When we invest in our own growth, we spark a chain reaction—transforming our communities and inspiring our youth to reimagine education as a dynamic journey of skill and creativity. Together, we can create a future defined by adaptability, innovation, and the enduring strength of our collective craftsmanship.

No matter our age or circumstances, the most American thing we can do is to learn and teach skills, hold the line on our individual autonomy, and begin to *close the trade gap* through the pursuit of hard things.

ABOUT THE AUTHOR

Zach Hanson is an avid hunter, trapper, and trade advocate. He is an expert in artificial intelligence and machine-learning product management, with experience developing AI solutions for Fortune 500 companies including IBM, Brightcove, Capital One, Genesys, and Wells Fargo. He holds degrees from the College of Charleston and Johns Hopkins University. He lives with his wife and three children at the base of the Sawtooth Mountains in Atlanta, Idaho.